# GREY OWL

JANE BILLINGHURST

FOREWORD BY DONALD B. SMITH

THE MANY FACES OF ARCHIE BELANEY

# GREY OWL

KODANSHA INTERNATIONAL
NEW YORK · TOKYO · LONDON

99 00 01 02 03   5 4 3 2 1

Kodansha America, Inc.
575 Lexington Avenue, New York, New York 10022 U.S.A

Kodansha International Ltd.
17-14 Otowa 1-chome, Bunkyo-ku, Tokyo 112-8652, Japan

Published in 1999 by Kodansha America, Inc.

*Library of Congress Cataloging-in-Publication Data*
Billinghurst, Jane, 1958–
Grey Owl : the many faces of Archie Belaney/Jane Billinghurst ;
foreword by Donald B. Smith
p.   cm.
Includes bibliographical references and index.
ISBN 1-56836-293-5
1. Grey Owl, 1888–1938.  2. Conservationists—Canada—Biography.
3. Indian philosophy—Canada.  4. Human ecology—Canada.  I. Title
E90.G75B55   1999
333.7′2′092—dc21
[B]                                                          99-20137

Editing by Nancy Flight
Jacket and text design by Peter Cocking
Front jacket photograph by W. J. Oliver,
Glenbow Archives, Calgary, Canada/NA-4868-213
Back jacket photograph courtesy Canadian Parks Service
Printed and bound in Canada on acid-free paper ∞

*To Stephanie and Nicola*

*for their patience and encouragement*

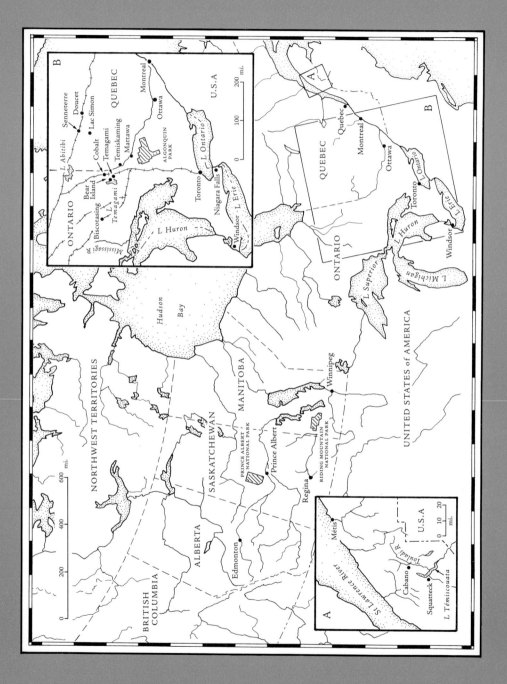

**Inset B** (top left):

B

L Abitibi
Senneterre
Doucet
Lac Simon
QUEBEC
ONTARIO
Cobalt
Temagami
Temiskaming
Mattawa
Montreal
Ottawa
ALGONQUIN PARK
Bear Island
L Temagami
Biscorasing
Mississagi R
L Huron
Toronto
L Ontario
Niagara Falls
Windsor
L Erie
U.S.A

200 mi.
100
0

**Main map:**

A
B
Quebec
Montreal
Ottawa
QUEBEC
Toronto
L Ontario
Windsor
L Erie
ONTARIO
L Superior
L Huron
L Michigan
Hudson Bay
UNITED STATES of AMERICA
NORTHWEST TERRITORIES
MANITOBA
Winnipeg
SASKATCHEWAN
PRINCE ALBERT NATIONAL PARK
Prince Albert
RIDING MOUNTAIN NATIONAL PARK
Regina
ALBERTA
Edmonton
BRITISH COLUMBIA

600 mi.
400
200
0

**Inset A** (bottom right):

A
St Lawrence River
Métis
Toulada R
Cabano
Squatteck
L Témiscouata
U.S.A

20 mi.
10
0

# Contents

# Foreword

IT WAS MARCH 26, 1938, at Toronto's Massey Hall, the largest performance hall in Canada. Before nearly three thousand people, the tall, hawk-faced man gave one of the best lectures of his life. Throughout he repeated: "Remember, you belong to Nature, not it to you." Since October 1937 he had spoken in Britain, Canada, and the United States to more than a quarter of a million people, including, at Buckingham Palace, the young princesses, Elizabeth and Margaret. His lectures, four books, and films with the beavers had made him one of the best-known Canadians of the 1930s.

Grey Owl lived at Beaver Lodge in Saskatchewan's Prince Albert National Park. He shared the small cabin with the beavers, which had built their lodge partly outside the cabin and partly inside. In early April the "beaver man" returned home, totally exhausted and run down. For more than half a year he had given all his physical and emotional strength to his crusade for conservation. Three days later park wardens rushed him to hospital in Prince Albert. The man believed to be the son of a Scot guide for Buffalo Bill and the Scot's Apache wife died on April 13.

Then came the bombshell. Swift detective work on both sides of the Atlantic in the following week allowed reporters to discover that Canada's best-known "Indian" was actually one Archie Belaney, born and raised in Hastings, England. In *Grey Owl: The Many Faces of Archie Belaney* Jane Billinghurst tells the fascinating story of this Englishman's re-invention of himself. But as she makes clear there is far more to the man than his masquerade.

Over sixty years after his death, his conservationist philosophy and his concern for the environment remain as timely as ever. Reading this biography reminds us that individuals can make a difference. The text, the quotes from his writings, and the photos bring alive the story, and the message, of one of Canada's earliest champions of conservation.

Having spent many hours in the early 1970s researching the life of this extraordinary man, in preparation for writing *From the Land of Shadows: The Making of Grey Owl*, I read this manuscript with great interest. While reading the text, I recalled many distant memories of interviews a quarter of a century ago with those who had known Grey Owl well. One of Jane Billinghurst's well-chosen quotes by Grey Owl struck me hardest: "And as I sit before my door of evenings and ponder these imponderable things, my mind turns sometimes to reminiscence … and I smell again the smoke of long-dead fires and see the images of faces and of figures that have forever vanished, seem to catch once more the sound of voices I'll never hear again."

DONALD B. SMITH
CALGARY, ALBERTA

*Facing page:* When the story broke that Grey Owl was not an Indian but an Englishman from Hastings, a former neighbor wondered, "How did the soul of an Indian find its way into a British boy?"

PART ONE

# The Lure of
# the Wild

A YOUNG MAN stands on a street of terraced houses in the seaside resort of Hastings, England. He has just turned sixteen; the year is 1904. In the predawn light he hoots once, like an owl. An upstairs window in one of the houses cautiously opens. The boy quickly shimmies up the drainpipe and disappears inside.

Archie Belaney has just made an early-morning visit to his friend George McCormick. They have planned a day of adventure in the Sussex countryside. Perhaps they will stalk wild animals in the style of the "Red Indians" they have read about in books. Perhaps they will add to the beaver dam they are creating in the stream that flows through nearby St. Helen's Woods. Or perhaps they will practice knife throwing at the lumberyard where Archie has just taken a job as a clerk.

Adventure stories have always captured the imaginations of young boys, but for Archie tales of the North American frontier provided more than just a temporary escape. Archie had no mother or father at home, an unusual situation for the times and one that he needed to explain, both to himself and to his friends. He knew his father was in America, and he knew from the stories on the bookshelves at home that men on the frontier were dashing and brave. It seemed the perfect place for an absent father to be. In Archie's mind, however, the young son of this brave Indian-fighter belonged not with those who had come to take the West but with those who already lived there. In a time when the cowboys always won, Archie wanted to be an Indian.

From the age of two Archie had lived in his grandmother's house, his upbringing entrusted to the vigilant attention of his father's two unmarried sisters, Carrie and Ada Belaney. George Furmage Belaney, Archie's father, had been a spendthrift and an alcoholic. George was the eldest of three children born into a wealthy, upper-middle-class English family. When he was twenty-four, unbeknownst to his family, he married a fifteen-year-

old girl pregnant with his child. Some time after the baby was born, he left behind both mother and daughter and then went to the United States with a young woman named Elizabeth Cox. When Elizabeth died a few years later, he married her fifteen-year-old sister, Kittie. By this time George was nearly thirty and had yet to show himself capable of supporting a family, and he was going through his mother's fortune at an alarming rate. Short of funds and leaving behind a child thought to be his daughter with Elizabeth, he returned to Hastings with his pregnant young wife.

*Facing page:* Kittie Belaney *(inset)*, Archie's mother, age thirty. Archie was raised by his father's sisters, Ada *(top left)* and Carrie *(top right)* Belaney. With neither parent in the home, he was free to reinvent his immediate family history.

Archibald Stansfeld Belaney was born on September 18, 1888. He lived with George and Kittie until Kittie became pregnant again. George's mother and sisters had never had much faith in George and Kittie's parenting abilities. As long as George and Kittie lived in Hastings, they could keep an eye on young Archie; but now, with a new child on the way, George and his family moved to the neighboring town of Deal. The Belaney sisters decided Archie would be better off in their care in Hastings, and Archie went to live with them in his grandmother's house. Although George made an effort to give up his drinking, his attempts at reform fell short. He continued to depend heavily on his mother for money, and eventually the elder Mrs. Belaney and her daughters decided that he was too much of a drain on the family resources. Kittie would be provided for as long as she agreed not to communicate with George. George was given a modest allowance and packed off to North America, where he died, reputedly in a drunken brawl, sometime before World War I. Archie hardly knew his father at all, and apart from sporadic visits when he was growing up, he spent little time with his mother and his younger brother, Hugh. He became, to all intents and purposes, an only child.

Life in the matriarchy in which Archie grew up was regimented and circumscribed. Aunt Ada oversaw his activities in the home, monitoring his every movement—from how often he brushed his teeth to how often he practiced the piano. She kept a small cane handy to rap his knuckles if he made a mistake at the keyboard, and although Archie was left-handed, Ada would not allow him to touch a pen or pencil with his left hand. If he did, she would pull him up out of his chair by his hair. He was so frustrated by her vigilant attention that he once tried to dislodge a plaster bust from a pedestal onto her head. His plan backfired and he knocked himself out instead.

To escape his Aunt Ada's attempts to turn him into a better man than his father had been, Archie immersed himself in a life of private adventure, devouring the nature stories of Ernest Thompson Seton and the adventure stories of James Fenimore Cooper. He soaked up information about North American Indians, sketching Indians in the margins of his books. When he was not reading, he was roaming St. Helen's Woods, a woodland

*Facing page:* Archie at the age of three. The mischievous twinkle in his eye would later be manifested in his sometimes unruly behavior on the Canadian frontier and in the touch of humor that was to make his nature writings so appealing.

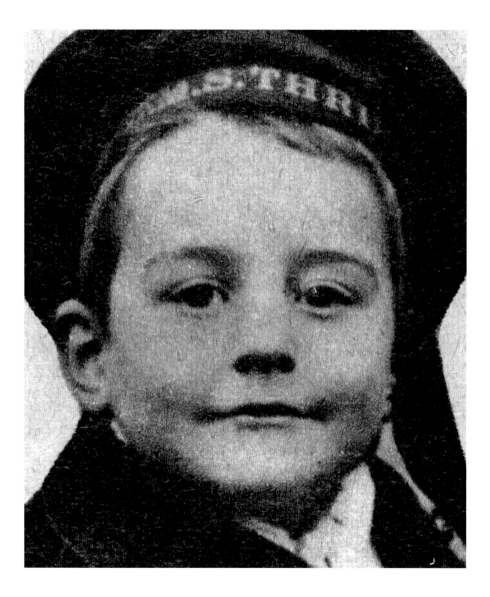

8   *Grey Owl*

area not far from his home, where he collected animals for his menagerie in the attic. Although she was strict in other ways, Ada indulged Archie's love of animals, allowing him to bring them into the house over her older sister's protestations—Carrie found the idea of snakes on the loose in the living room unnerving.

At school Archie excelled in English, French, and religious knowledge. He put his knowledge of chemistry to good use, often setting off unauthorized explosions. He had a habit of carrying reptiles and other small creatures around in his pockets, much to the delight of some pupils and to the horror of his teachers. In the school yard, he organized a gang of Red Indians (as the English called North American Indians in those days) that carried out raids on enemies and laid plans to scalp unsuspecting parents. Some of the boys at school took to calling him "Squaw Man," which they understood to be a term of contempt.

*Facing page:* Archie at the age of thirteen. Aunt Ada was busy molding Archie into the young gentleman she wished him to become, but beneath this polished exterior seethed an imagination steeped in stories of the American Wild West.

In 1903, a month before Archie turned fifteen, Buffalo Bill's Wild West Show rode into town, complete with "Indians of the type familiarized by the illustrations which grace the cover of the penny 'blood and thunder' publication." The show made a deep impression on Archie. Not only did it provide him with a lasting image of what "real" Indians looked like, it also gave him more material for his imagined life. His father, he decided, disgusted with the wars against the Indians, had joined the show and

# Neganikabo

*Archie learned much of the ways of the wilderness from the Bear Island Ojibway in northern Ontario. Neganikabo appears in a number of Archie's later writings as a repository of Indian lore and wisdom. His name translates as Man That Stands Ahead or Stands First. The character is likely a composite of the Ojibway elders Old Misabi and Ned White Bear, otherwise known as Temagami Ned.*

NEGANIKABO, MY MENTOR, my kindly instructor, my companion in untold hardship and nameless tribulation, has pulled back little by little, the magic invisible veil of mystery from across the face of the forest, that I might learn its uttermost secrets, and has laid open before me the book of Nature for me to read; and in my bungling way I have profited from his lessons, but the half is not yet done.

*Facing page:* Temagami Ned (*right*) was a great favorite with the tourists who came to Lake Temagami, Ontario, to fish and hunt game. Old Misabi (*left*) was reputed to be over one hundred years old when Archie got to know him.

I have followed him when snowshoes sank into the soft snow halfway to the knee, mile after weary mile, to sleep at night behind a square of canvas; this for five days and nights, it snowing steadily most of the time, and with nothing to eat but strips of dried moose-meat, and teas made from boiled leaves of the Labrador sage. I have negotiated dangerous rapids under his tuition, when at each run, after the irrevocable step of entering, I doubted much that I would make the foot alive. He has led me [on] many hours

12　Grey Owl

of travel with birch bark flares at night, and more than once entire nights in an unknown country without them. . . .

His faculties of observation, as with most Indians, were very keen; nothing seemed to escape him. He could detect game invisible to me, yet his gaze was not piercing, rather it was comprehensive, all-embracing, effortless, as is the eye of a camera, registering every detail in a moment of time. He often made fire with bow and spindle, habitually carried flint and steel, and seemed to have knowledge of the speech of some animals, calling them almost at will in the right season. He carried a beaded pouch which contained, among other trinkets, some small beaver bones. . . . He showed me, in the course of years, did I but have the head to hold it all, what a man may learn in a long life of observation and applied experience.

*Facing page:* In becoming Grey Owl, Archie combined what he learned from the Ojibway with the romantic image of the Indians of his youth to create an image complete with buckskins, beads, and eagle feather.

*Archie imagines that Neganikabo summons him to lay the old man to rest at the end of his life:* I buried him the next day in his old canoe, with his muzzle-loading gun, his old-fashioned axe, and his beaded pouch of relics by his side, in the smooth ground beneath the birches near the lake-shore. . . .

And there he will always be, facing towards the West, so that the rays of the setting sun to which he turned so wistfully in his last moments, may, at the close of every summer day, bathe his resting-place, in the Glory of his Sunset Trail.

traveled to England with his young son, who spent nine months in England performing and acquiring an education.

Archie left school in July 1904, a couple of months before his sixteenth birthday, and entered the employ of Cheale Brothers, lumber merchants, where he worked as a clerk. He continued to pursue his interest in Indians. Already a good shot (he once unerringly shot rats that were eating scraps set out for a neighbor's chickens), he now taught himself how to throw knives, and he continued to announce his presence at the neighbors' with his trademark hoot of an owl. He did not take well to the restrictions of office life, however, and he was summarily dismissed after setting off a small but effective explosion in the office chimney.

For years Archie had been preparing himself for something more than a desk job in a sleepy seaside town. Ever since he was a young boy, he had had dreams about the American West. Now Archie decided it was time to try on his fantasy life for size. He would go to North America and see for himself what he had so far experienced only through books, traveling shows, and make-believe. His aunts were reluctant to let him leave, but the incident at the lumberyard had convinced them that it was time for their young nephew to expand his horizons. Ada accompanied Archie on the train journey from Hastings to Liverpool via London. On March 29, 1906, Archie Belaney boarded the ss *Canada* bound for Halifax, Nova Scotia, eager to embrace whatever he found.

Whatever Archie was seeking, he did not find it in his first position in Canada. It is likely that he traveled from Halifax to

Toronto, where, it is believed, he toiled for a few months in the men's furnishings department at Eaton's. He then took advantage of the recent silver strike at Cobalt in northern Ontario to ride the rails to the frontier. He was not interested in silver, however. What he was looking for was a place where he could live his dreams.

When Archie got off the train, a young man totally inexperienced in the ways of the bush, he was lucky enough to be directed to Bill Guppy. Bill Guppy was a seasoned bushman who, along with his brothers, Alex and George, made his living helping the wealthy sports hunters and fishermen who came to the area to unwind from the pressures of city life. Bill took the greenhorn under his wing, and Archie spent the winter at Lake Temiskaming with Bill and his family, learning how to trap and snowshoe and honing his knife-throwing skills. In May 1907 Archie made the long trek with the Guppys by canoe and portage to the tourist lodge at Lake Temagami. Bear Island, in the center of the lake, was the summer home of about one hundred Ojibway. Here at last were the wilderness and the people that Archie had traveled so far to find.

The Guppys hired out as guides from the Temagami Inn. Archie did not have the experience to hire out as a guide, but he did find work doing chores at the inn. At the end of the summer, the Guppys and the Indians returned to their respective hunting grounds. Archie applied to the manager of the Hudson's Bay Company trading post for a grubstake to go trapping but was turned down because of his inexperience. Discouraged, he returned briefly to England, probably to obtain funds from his aunts. His first foray into life on the frontier had not been a resounding success, but he was determined not to give up.

The summer of 1908 found Archie back doing chores at the Temagami Inn. In this isolated district, where no one knew of his past, he let it be known that he was a "half-breed." He told people that he had spent his boyhood in the American Southwest, that his mother was an Apache, and that he had traveled in his youth with Buffalo Bill's Wild West Show. Whether people cared about his origins or believed his story is unknown. To the Ojibway, he was a tall, lanky Englishman with brown hair and blue eyes who stood out from the Indians just as a tree marked with a blaze stands out in the forest. It was obvious that he had a lot to learn.

And learn is just what Archie was here to do.

*Facing page:* Archie lived in the bush with John Egwuna and his family for a season before marrying John's niece Angele. Archie said he would make a white woman out of her. "Oh no, Archie," she replied, "I make the Indian of you."

In the kitchen of the Temagami Inn Archie met Angele Egwuna. Angele was young, she was strong, and she was beautiful. She was also greatly attracted to this strange young Englishman. As Angele spoke no English and Archie spoke no Ojibway, at first the young couple communicated by sign language. Angele was at home in this land that Archie was so eager to learn about, and she showed him how the Ojibway set traps and fishing nets. She also introduced him to other members of the Bear Island Band. Here was the opening that Archie had been patiently waiting for—an opportunity to learn from the Indians themselves. He was a dedicated and attentive pupil, aware

18    *Grey Owl*

perhaps that the Indian way of life that these people embodied, that he had spent his childhood preparing for, and that he had traveled so far to find was in danger of disappearing.

Angele's uncle John Egwuna gave Archie the name Ko-hom-see, or Little Owl, because he sat and looked and listened, taking in everything. In the winter of 1909–10, the Egwunas invited Archie to spend the winter trapping with them. Archie chose to remember what he was later to describe as his adoption by the Ojibway people in slightly different terms. His version of events included an induction ceremony in which an Ojibway medicine man danced to the beat of Indian drums accompanied by the wailing of reed pipes and skirring of

*Facing page:* Angele, Agnes, and the postmaster in Biscotasing, Ontario. Archie left Angele when Agnes was a year old, returning to her briefly after the war. It was Angele who finally revealed Archie's true identity to the world.

turtle shell rattles around an open fire. As a large group of Ojibway chanted in almost-forgotten cadences, the flames threw shadows across the lower branches of the surrounding pines. After Archie had stepped into the circle of faces and received his new name, the chanting transformed itself into the hollow, prolonged hoot of an owl, whose name he now bore. Although Archie's version strayed from events as others remembered them, his fanciful narrative accurately described the sense of kinship he was to feel for these Indians for the rest of his life.

In the summer of 1910, Archie was twenty-one years old, and he had found the Indians he had been looking for. On August 23 he married Angele, and the following spring their daughter Agnes

# $\mathcal{F}$IRE RANGING

*In later years when Archie was employed by the Canadian Parks
Branch and could no longer travel freely, he sat in his cabin on the shores
of Lake Ajawaan in Prince Albert National Park in Saskatchewan
and conjured up memories of the companions and adventures of his
fire-ranging days in Biscotasing, Ontario.*

AND AS I SIT before my door of evenings and ponder these
imponderable things, my mind turns sometimes to
reminiscence . . . and I smell again the smoke of long-dead fires
and see the images of faces and of figures that have forever
vanished, seem to catch once more the sound of voices I'll never
hear again. Familiar hands, rough, kind and
friendly, paddle-calloused and strong, seem to
reach towards me from the past. A host of
small, companionable creatures, bright-eyed,
curious and pathetic, tiny guests at a thousand
camp grounds, come rustling through the dry
leaves with a welcome, as I commence my
march back down the avenues of Time. . . .

*Facing page:* Archie was a quick
learner. He soon became skilled with
the paddle, and he was proud of his
ability to survive in the wilderness. He
felt far more comfortable in the bush
than he had ever felt in civilization.

So, speed, speed, speed, grip the canoe ribs with your knees, drive
those paddles deep, throw your weight onto them, click them on
those gunnels twenty-five strokes to the minute; spurn that water
in gurgling eddies behind you, bend those backs, and drive! . . .

The spruce trees look like witches with tall, pointed bonnets and sable cloaks, and the white birches that flicker here and there among them as we pass, shine whitely out like slim, attenuated skeletons and in the shifting, garish moonbeams seem gruesomely to dance. . . .

And down its mad course go the Rivermen, carefree and debonair, wild, reckless, and fancy-free, gay caballeros riding the hurricane deck, rocketing down the tossing foaming River; a gallant, colourful array, my trail companions; Men of the Mississauga.

But I am dropping behind—I cannot catch up, I cannot follow—What is this?—they are leaving me!

And now suddenly the canoes slip silently, swiftly away on the dark bosom of the River; the figures of the paddlers dwindle, become dim and disappear, and the sound of their singing is gone. The sound of the waters recedes, fades away—

Silence.

An old poling-iron and a faded photograph are on the table before me. In my hand is not a paddle, but a pen. I am alone.

The stove is cold and pale Dawn creeps in through the window. Faintly, from somewhere outside, there comes the clear, poignantly beautiful carolling of a white-throat. Ah, I remember now, the bird I heard so often in the nighttime; the Requiem.

I have spent a night with the Lost Brigade.

was born. Since Archie now had a wife and daughter to support, he spent the summers of 1910 and 1911 working as a guide at Camp Keewaydin, a camp for eleven- and twelve-year-old American prep school boys. Here the boys learned to fish and canoe and played at being Indians. The boys' childish enthusiasm brought home to Archie the gap between dreams and reality. In Archie's case, after three years of living with the Ojibway, the initial excitement of living as an Indian was beginning to wear off, and there was the added complication of having a child. Not only was Archie struggling to reconcile his fantasies about Indian life with the life he was actually living, he was also struggling with the concept of taking responsibility for others. He had no parental role model to follow and found himself at a loss.

Archie's solution to his dilemma was to distance himself from Angele and Agnes and from the lifestyle they represented. In the fall of 1911, he left his wife and daughter and joined three other white trappers in Abitibi on the border between Ontario and Quebec. He sent written accounts of his trapping adventures back to Hastings, where they were published in his old school magazine, the *Hastonian*. He wrote that he acted as the interpreter for the group because he could "murder the beautiful flowing gutturals and meat-axe noises made by the red brother." Despite the warm welcome extended to him by Angele and her band, Archie was slipping into the role of the superior white man.

After a few months trapping in Abitibi, Archie most likely spent the rest of the winter in Toronto. It was clear from his correspondence that life in the bush was not the romantic adventure he had thought it would be. He described being bitten day and night by insects, getting soaked in pouring rain and burned up with heat, dragging a loaded toboggan through the snow, and sleeping out in 60 or 70 degrees below zero. But Archie Belaney did not give up easily. Despite the physical discomforts of life in the bush, he was determined not to abandon the North. He would give it another try. This time, however, he decided to do it unencumbered by family ties.

In the summer of 1912, Archie Belaney appeared in the logging town of Biscotasing in northern Ontario. The town had a sawmill, a railway station, and a Hudson's Bay Company post. In Biscotasing, Archie got a summer job with the Ontario Forestry Branch as a fire ranger in the nearby Mississaga Forest Reserve. He did not return to his wife and young child, although he did send them money from his ranger's wages and the checks he was receiving from his aunts back in England.

Gradually Archie became acclimatized to life in the North, and he began to take considerable pride in his accomplishments. In his first book, *The Men of the Last Frontier*, he described bushmen who had lost their bearings in the wilderness and never made it out alive. In *Tales of an Empty Cabin*, he proudly stated that he had never been lost, but he did admit to having been "turned around" on more than one occasion. He described crossing and re-crossing his own tracks one dark night convinced he was following the trail of an ever-increasing party of people. Later in the same book, he described the gut-wrenching hunger he had once experienced on the trail, when he was so hungry that he had been glad to eat the rancid marrow from the bones of a long-dead moose. On another occasion he was so desperate that he had thawed and toasted some partridge intestines rejected by an owl. With his trademark self-deprecating humor he noted that he could not recommend the meal to others.

Years later, Woody Cowper, a fellow ranger, said that in those early days in Biscotasing Archie was "considered a white man, with possibly a streak of Indian in him." Constantly exposed to the elements, his skin was becoming darker, and he wore his hair down to his shoulders, using two strands of trolling line to keep it out of his eyes. He carried around notebooks in which he jotted down observations of life around him, and he began to cultivate a relationship with alcohol. One of his bosses at the time, Bill Draper, remembers firing Archie and another fire ranger, Baptiste Commanda, after he caught them dead drunk while supposedly in charge of a fire ranger's camp. Bill worked with Archie a few years later, however, and did not hold the incident against him. Bill had been known to take a drink or two himself. "Please excuse me, it's my birthday," Bill would say on those occasions that alcohol got the better of him. Archie told Bill that he had spent time in his youth fighting in New Mexico and that his father was a Texas Ranger who had met with a violent end.

*Facing page:* Archie was a sniper on the Western Front in World War I. While convalescing in England, he married his second wife, Ivy Holmes, neglecting to mention to her that he already had an Ojibway wife back in Canada.

In the winter of 1912, Archie once again traveled south, this time to Toronto and Montreal, returning to Biscotasing the following summer. Unable to bring himself to return to his wife and child, he started a relationship with Marie Girard, a Métis woman who worked as a maid at the boardinghouse in Bisco. Archie met Marie one day when he was having an early breakfast at the boardinghouse. She came into the dining room with a tray full of cutlery, which she proceeded to throw up into the air. Archie joined in her laughter as it all fell to the floor. Marie was fired and Archie invited her to join him on his trapline for the winter of 1913–14. Marie agreed.

In the summer of 1914, Archie was again working as a fire ranger in the Mississaga reserve. He continued to embellish his Indian past. He let it be known that his mother was an Apache and his father was a Scot, that he had been born in Mexico, and that he had grown up in the ways of the Plains Indians in the American Southwest. He acknowledged that while he was traveling with Buffalo Bill's Wild West Show he had spent time in the south of England, where his father's two sisters had seen to it that he got an education. He became known as Anaquoness, an Ojibway word he translated as 'Little Hat,' because of the Mexican sombrero he wore.

On his return to Bisco at the end of the 1914 fire-ranging season, Archie got drunk, trashed the lumber company's boardinghouse, and promptly went into hiding. He emerged in mid-November to go out on the trapline again with Marie. It is likely that he left Marie in January 1915, perhaps because she was pregnant and he was in horror of once again being responsible for a woman and her child. Whatever the cause of his departure, on May 6, 1915, he enlisted in the Canadian army in Digby, Nova Scotia, making no mention of a wife or dependents. On enlistment, Archie claimed to have had previous military experience with the Mexican Scouts, 28th Dragoons. On the strength of that "previous military experience," he was made a lance-corporal. In mid-June he sailed for England.

When Archie arrived in England, he went absent without leave to visit his aunts in Hastings. As a result he was demoted to private. To his fellow soldiers, he was half Indian, born in Mexico, a country he claimed he had had to flee after shooting the man responsible for killing his brother. Archie was assigned to the 13th Battalion of the Royal Highlanders of Canada, today known as the Canadian Black Watch, and he was sent to war in late August 1915 wearing a kilt. The battalion was holding the front in trenches at Ypres Salient. Because Archie was more of a loner than a team player, he was made a sniper-observer. He was known as a patient field observer and an excellent shot. He was also known to drink. One fellow sniper reported that after Archie and his sniping partner drank "firewater" they acted like a pair of half-crazy half-breeds.

Archie was away from the front for two weeks in January 1916 to recover from a wrist wound and for a month in March when he attended a sniper's course. There were violent clashes with

# The Forest

*It is clear from this description of the winter forest that Archie possessed a vivid imagination.*

BEAUTIFUL AS THIS Arctic forest appears in the daytime, it is only by moonlight, when much travelling is done to avoid the cutting winds of the daylight hours, that the true witchery of the winter wilderness grips the imagination. See by the eerie light of the moon, the motionless, snow-shrouded trees that line the trail, loom on either hand like grim spectres, gruesomely arrayed, each in his winding-sheet, staring sardonically down on the hurrying wayfarer. In the diffused uncertain light the freakish artistry of the wind appears like the work of some demented sculptor, and the trail becomes a gallery of grinning masks and uncouth featureless forms, as of dwellers in a world of goblins turned to stone.

Athwart the shafts of moonlight, from out the shadows, move soundless forms with baleful gleaming eyes, wraiths that flicker before the vision for a moment and are gone. The Canada lynx, great grey ghost of the Northland; the huge white Labrador wolf; white rabbits, white weasels, the silvery ptarmigan: pale phantoms of the white silence. A phantasy in white in a world that is dead.

And in the moonlight, too, is death. The full of the moon is the period of most intense cold, and there have been men who, already exhausted by a day's travel, and carrying on by night, half-asleep as they walked, their senses lulled by the treacherous glow, decided to sleep for just a little while on a warm-looking snow bank, and so slept on forever. So Muji-Manito, the Evil Genius of the North, cold and pitiless, malignantly triumphant, adds another victim to his gruesome tally.

Then later, when the moon has set, in that stark still hour between the darkness and the dawn, the snow gives back the pale sepulchral glare of the Northern Lights; and by their unearthly illumination, those who dance the Dance of the Deadmen [the Northern Lights] perform their ghostly evolutions, before the vast and solemn audience of spruce.

And then the stillness is broken by the music of the wolves, whose unerring instinct senses tragedy. It comes, a low moaning, stealing through the thin and brittle air, swelling in crescendo to a volume of sound, then dying away in a sobbing wail across the empty solitudes; echoing from hill to hill in fading repetition, until the reiteration of sound is lost in the immensity of immeasurable distance.

And as the last dying echo fades to nothing, the silence settles down layer by layer, pouring across the vast deserted auditorium in billow after billow, until all sound is completely choked beyond apparent possibility of repetition. And the wolves move on to their ghastly feast, and the frozen wastes resume their endless waiting; the Deadmen dance their grisly dance on high, and the glittering spruce stand silently and watch.

the Germans in Ypres Salient in April, and on April 23 Archie Belaney was wounded in the foot and sent back to England. Almost a year later, in March 1917 at the London General Hospital, the fourth toe of his right foot was removed. The injury never completely healed, and when he returned to Canada his foot often bothered him on the trail. After his death, his missing toe was positive identification that he was Archie Belaney.

Archie told his nurse at the King George Hospital in London, where he spent the first four months after being returned from the front, that his mother was an Apache Indian and his father was a Scot. He abandoned his Indian identity, however, when he renewed his acquaintance with a childhood friend, Ivy Holmes.

Ivy's mother shared Aunt Ada's interest in raising purebred collie dogs, and the two children had spent time together in Hastings and at the Holmes's apartment in Hammersmith. When he was young, Archie had tried to impress Ivy with the snakes he had kept in the attic, and the two of them had visited London Zoo together. In 1917, at twenty-six, Ivy was attractive, intelligent, well traveled, and single. She had studied ballet in London, and before the war she had been to Europe with a professional dance and acting troupe. She listened eagerly to Archie's stories of Canada and encouraged him to put his impressions of the wilderness down on paper. As the two of them took walks in the countryside, she shared with him her experiences

*Facing page:* Ivy Holmes around 1915. Archie and Ivy were married for seven months before Archie returned to Canada alone; Ivy never saw him again. She divorced him in 1921, when he told her of Angele's existence.

34   *Grey Owl*

in Russia, Budapest, and Constantinople. One day, when they were passing an especially picturesque church just outside Hastings, they decided to get married. The ceremony took place on February 10, 1917, even though Archie was still legally married to Angele.

What could Archie have been thinking of? Perhaps he felt that his wounded foot would make life in the bush impossible and he was contemplating settling down in England. He was still in the Canadian army, however, and as long as he was a Canadian soldier, to Canada he must return. On September 19, 1917, Archie sailed for Canada. Ivy stayed behind in England to wait out the war.

*Facing page:* Alex Espaniel was the closest thing to a father that Archie ever knew. The Espaniels taught Archie how to trap and to respect nature. In return, he taught their daughter, Jane, to write English.

That fall, doctors in Toronto examined Archie's foot and declared him medically unfit to be a soldier; he was discharged in November 1917 and returned to Bisco. Despite his war wound, he seems to have had no serious plans to trade the raw edge of the Canadian frontier for the well-ordered hedgerows and fields of the British countryside. Now that he was on his way to the place he had decided to call home, he must have wondered how he could ever bring Ivy to northern Ontario. He already had an Indian wife and child in Temagami and, last he had heard, a girl-friend and possibly another child waiting for him in Bisco. And how could he reconcile the Archie that Ivy knew with the half-breed he portrayed himself as in Bisco? In the end, he never sent for Ivy, and she never came.

When Archie returned to Bisco in the fall of 1917, he learned that Marie Girard had borne him a child, Johnny Jero, on September 16, 1915, and that she had died of tuberculosis shortly afterwards. The local midwife, Edith Langevin, a Cree, had taken the boy under her wing. Archie decided to leave things well enough alone, and it was not until Johnny was nine that he discovered that the man he knew as Archie Baloney was his father.

Archie visited Angele briefly in Temagami, but he did not stay. His life was a mess. He had abandoned his Ojibway wife, the woman who had introduced him to the Indian way of life he had so longed to know, and his Ojibway daughter; his Métis girlfriend and trapping partner and the son she was to bear him; and his English wife and childhood friend. These three completely different women pretty much reflected all aspects of his life so far: British upper-middle-class upbringing; yearnings for the lifestyle of the romanticized "Red Indian"; and frontier life on the trapline in the bush. Had these all been false starts? He desperately needed a new beginning.

*Facing page:* Archie made this Indian costume himself. When he left Biscotasing in 1925 he gave it to fur buyer Jack Leve, who won prizes with it at dress-up parties in Sudbury in the 1930s.

Archie began to drink hard, and he gained a reputation as a troublemaker. He drank whatever he could get his hands on: moonshine (which he made himself), boot polish, vanilla extract. He took to beating drums and singing strange songs that he thought sounded Indian, though none of the Cree or Ojibway in the area had ever heard them before. Perhaps if he

# THE TRAPPER

*Although as the famous North American Indian conservationist Grey Owl, Archie Belaney was to renounce the life of a trapper, he always treasured the independence and self-reliance he learned in following this way of life, and he always prized life in the bush far above life in civilization.*

HE WHO LEADS the precarious life of skirmisher or scout on the No-Man's-Land beyond the Frontier, becomes so imbued with the spirit of his environment, that when the advance guard of the new era sweeps down on him with its flow of humanity and modern contrivance, he finds he cannot adapt himself to the new conditions. Accustomed to loneliness and seclusion, when his wanderings are curtailed, he forthwith gathers his few belongings and, like the Arab, folds his tent and steals silently away. Thus he moves on, stage by stage, with his furred and feathered associates, to fresh untrammelled horizons; where he explores, lays his trails, and unearths secret places to his heart's content, blazing the way for civilization, and again retiring before it when it comes. . . .

*Facing page: A display of furs in the 1920s. By the time Archie started to trap, fur-bearing animals were already on the wane in northern Ontario.*

In tune with his surroundings, wise in the lore of the Indian, he reads and correctly interprets the cryptograms in the book that lies open before him, scanning the face of Nature and forestalling her moods to his advantage. Dependent entirely on himself, he must be resourceful, ready to change plan at a moment's notice,

turning adverse circumstances and reverses to what slight
advantage he may. The hardships and privations of the trapper's
life have developed in him a determination, a dogged
perseverance, and a bulldog tenacity of purpose not often
necessary in other walks of life. . . .

He scans the face of the wilderness, and there
gets his inspiration. The pale disc of the moon
shining through the interlaced limbs of a
leafless tree; the silhouette of tall distant pines
against the frosty sky; the long shadows cast by
a winter sunset across the white expanse of a
snow-bound lake, all strike a chord which finds a ready response
in his breast. He may not be able, or willing, to express his
feelings to the world, but they indubitably impress his unspoken
thoughts. The sublimity, the immensity, and the silent majesty
of his surroundings influence his character, and the trapper
is often a quiet thoughtful man, set in his ways, and not overly
given to conversation. . . .

*Facing page:* A 58-pound beaver trapped near Biscotasing in 1925. Before he worked to conserve beavers, Archie regularly trapped them.

An anachronism, belonging to a day long past, he marches back
down the avenues of time, a hundred years in as many steps.
With a glance at the sun for direction, and eye to the lie of the
land easiest for his dogs, feeling for signs of an unseen and drifted
trail with his feet, he swings along on his big snow-shoes, out
across the Frontier, beyond the ken of mortal man, to be no more
seen in the meagre civilization he has left behind.

pounded on those drums hard enough, they would drown out the unwelcome noises the rest of his life was making.

The pine-covered expanses of northern Ontario, which once had beckoned him with their romantic allure, now became his escape. He had never much liked civilization, and after his experiences in the war he wanted even less to do with it. In Bisco, Archie went back to working as a fire ranger in the summer and trapping in the winter. In 1921 he finally told Ivy about Angele, and Ivy immediately served him with divorce papers.

*Facing page:* Archie, Bill Miller, and Jim Espaniel perform a war dance. In Biscotasing, dressing up was a popular pastime. With his flair for the dramatic, Archie entered wholeheartedly into the spirit of things.

In the early 1920s Archie got as close as he ever came to having a father figure in his life. He lived for two or three summers with the Ojibway family of Alex and Anny Espaniel, joining them on their trapping grounds for two winters. He came to call Alex "the one I am proud to call 'Dad', & who taught me much of whatever I may know." Archie kept Alex up into the small hours talking about the Ojibway way of life. He used Anny's Roman Catholic prayer book to expand his Ojibway vocabulary. Under their patient tutelage he discovered the values of conservation, and they severely reprimanded him when he undertook such outrages as once dynamiting a beaver lodge. Archie was an assiduous pupil and a quick study. At home and out on the trail he took copious notes, drew sketches, and worked on stories. Archie was beginning to regain his equilibrium and was once again enthusiastically learning to be an Indian.

Archie started to change his appearance, dyeing his hair black with No Tox dye and coloring his skin brown with henna. He worked hard to form his features into a stern, Indian-looking face, practicing for hours in front of the mirror. He made himself an elaborate Indian costume from brown cotton purchased at the lumber company's store. He perfected his own style of Indian war dance, in which some members of the community participated. On May 23, 1923, Archie orchestrated a command performance of the dance for the town's Victoria Day celebration. The event was even written up in the Sudbury paper.

Under the instruction of Alex Espaniel, Archie learned to be a better trapper. He reveled in his newfound knowledge and in life beyond the reach of civilization. He prided himself on his skill in living off the land. A loner since his boyhood days in Hastings, he found that the solitary life on the trapline suited his character. There he could pit himself against nature and gain satisfaction in knowing that he could survive where many men could not. He was indebted to the Indians for the knowledge they had shared with him, and he would never forget the debt he owed them.

He still had his problems with civilization. In April 1925 there was a warrant out for Archie's arrest for drunk and disorderly behavior at the Bisco train station. He had a habit of hooting at the trains like an owl and throwing knives at the boxcars as they steamed by. In July 1925 he decided it was time to get out of town.

Archie had achieved his childhood goal. The young boy who had tracked small animals in the confines of St. Helen's Woods now made his living guiding and trapping on the Canadian frontier. The question was, what now? Archie did not seem to know. In the summer of 1925 he tried returning to Angele and Agnes. At the age of thirty-six, however, Archie still had a horror of family life, and he left Angele before his second daughter with her, Flora, was born. Angele never saw him again, although she did recognize his photograph in the local paper when he became famous. The newspaper that followed up on her story broke the news, one day after Archie's death, that the famed Grey Owl was a fraud. In the summer of 1925, however, Archie, ever the wanderer, was still searching for something. Then, in late summer, on the shores of Lake Temagami, he found it.

PART TWO

# Anahareo and the Beaver People

IN LATE SUMMER 1925, Archie paddled his canoe up to the gravel beach at Camp Wabikon on Lake Temagami, where a young Iroquois woman was reading in the shade of the pines. Nineteen-year-old Gertrude Bernard—Pony to her friends—was working as a waitress to earn a little spending money before enrolling in a Roman Catholic boarding school in Toronto in the fall. Archie was back in Temagami earning money as a guide.

At the sound of the canoe being pulled up over the gravel, Pony looked up from her book. She saw a tall, handsome woodsman dressed in dark brown buckskins, who stepped out of his canoe with the speed and grace of a panther and then gazed wistfully across the lake in the direction from which he had come. His long hair and wide-brimmed hat reminded her of her childhood hero, Jesse James. She was determined to discover the identity of this romantic-looking stranger.

Pony lost no time finding out that Archie had been hired as a guide and that he had pitched his tent a short distance up the lake. Then she sat down on a bench by the trail that led to his camp and waited. Archie came down the trail and stopped dead in his tracks at the sight of this slender, dark beauty. His first words to her were: "Say, do you happen to have a bag of potatoes?" Over the next few weeks he courted Pony with the gawkishness of an adolescent, attracting her attention by shaking the bench they were both sitting on and cracking bad jokes in her presence. Their tentative advances to one another continued until Pony was called home to attend a family funeral. Archie visited her briefly at her father's house in nearby Mattawa and inundated her with long, lively letters, one of which ran to over one hundred pages. Archie Belaney was in love.

Fall came and it was time to set out trapping again. That year Archie was forced to move his trapping grounds from Ontario to Quebec. As the Indians' hunting grounds became increasingly devoid of game, the Ontario government passed a law forbidding non-Indians to trap fur-bearing animals in Ontario. Since Archie was not registered under the Indian Act, he had to move on. He went to Doucet in the Abitibi region of northwestern Quebec.

From his trapline, Archie continued to write Pony long letters, while his trapping partners helped to build a cabin for her in the hopes that she would abandon her plans to attend school and join Archie instead. Although Pony was Iroquois, she was town-bred and unfamiliar with life in the bush; Archie knew much more about life in the wilds than she did. In February 1926 she finally came, making the forty-mile hike from Doucet to the cabin on snowshoes without complaining, although she said of the first part of the trek: "After five hours of snowshoeing I was all but crawling on my eyebrows." When they finally reached the cabin she was enchanted with the dark green log walls, chinked with red, green, and yellow moss, the shining hair of the moose-hide rug, and the bunk fluffed high with balsam boughs and covered by a red Hudson's Bay blanket.

Although Archie never told Pony that he was not part Indian, that winter he did reveal to her details of his life that he had never told anyone else, including stories about his unrelenting Aunt Ada. Archie told her of Angele and of Ivy, but not of his true origins. He gave her the name Anahareo, which he derived from Naharrenou, the name of a Mohawk chief to whom Pony was distantly related.

Anahareo was enthralled with Archie's stories of his two wives. To her he was every bit as romantic as she had hoped he would be. The drama and excitement that drew her to him, however, also provided for some stormy times between them. In the spring, they traveled to Doucet. Here they checked into a hotel and Archie proceeded to whoop it up with other trappers coming to town after a winter in isolation. Anahareo felt ignored and decided she would get drunk herself. After drinking the better part of a bottle of whiskey in her room, she decided to fetch Archie's rifle and shoot the lot of them. Archie found her before she got to the gun and dissuaded her, explaining how difficult it would be to dig graves for all the bodies, as the town was built on bedrock.

Anahareo gave up the gun but didn't feel much better in the morning. She decided she would leave Archie and travel to the nearby town of Rouyn. Archie was furious and insisted that she either return home to her father or stay and marry him. When she said she didn't love him, he told her he was putting her on the night train home. Anahareo was so incensed that she grabbed Archie's hunting knife from his belt and stabbed him in the arm, drawing blood. She then ran screaming out of the hotel, and he had to run after her to calm her down.

*Facing page:* Anahareo was beautiful, impetuous, and independent. Over eighteen years Archie's junior, she was the love of his life. She stayed with him for eleven years, until his all-consuming drive to write finally drove her away.

Anahareo refused to leave her hotel room for the next three days. When she did come down it was to find Archie drunkenly dancing around a room twirling a dainty sun parasol while a fellow trapper jumped about wrapped in a white tablecloth. Anahareo decided she could not leave Archie in this state, and he was adamant that their ways should part, whereupon Anahareo burst into tears and told him she loved him. He embraced her and proposed that they get married. This level of passion would remain in their relationship until the end.

After a winter of trapping, Archie spent the summer of 1926 working in Quebec as a fire ranger. One day before he left for duty in his fire tower, he was approached by an Indian who requested his assistance. Two Indians were in jail for setting fire to a trappers' cabin. They had destroyed the cabin and the trappers' equipment because the two white men had used strychnine in poison baits— which was illegal—and the Indians' huskies, on whom they depended, had eaten the bait and died. Archie argued eloquently in court in favor of the Indians, and they received a greatly reduced sentence. Nias Papaté, the chief of the Lac Simon Band, invited Archie and Anahareo over to the band's encampment so that the Indians could express their gratitude to Archie, and while the couple were staying there, the chief declared them husband and wife.

In the winter of 1926–27, Anahareo again joined Archie on his trapline. This season she was not content to spend her time in the cabin, and so she accompanied Archie as he made his rounds. She was disgusted by what she saw. Nothing in her small-town upbringing had prepared her for the heart-wrenching sight of the frozen corpses of animals who had died in agony while trying desperately to escape from the unyielding metal jaws of the leghold traps. Nor could she bear to watch as Archie used the wooden handle of his axe to club to death those who were still living.

The grisly sights on the traplines moved Archie less than they moved his wife because he was used to them, but even he found it hard to take the barbaric methods of the recent onslaught of inexperienced white trappers who only wanted to make a quick profit and then move on. These trappers left many maimed and wounded animals to wander in the bush to die long, lingering deaths. They set spring poles for beavers that left the animals to die of thirst suspended just inches above a pond full of life-giving water. They caught beavers no matter what the season, including the spring, when the death of parents meant that orphaned kittens would certainly starve to death.

The wholesale slaughter by the new breed of trappers stood in sharp contrast to the trapping and harvesting techniques Archie had learned from Indians such as the Egwunas and the Espaniels. Archie's Indian hunting companions dealt the animals they caught a swift death. They performed ceremonies to honor the animals whose lives they took. They hung bear skulls in prominent places in the bears' former ranges, and they laid the bodies of skinned beaver in comfortable positions and burned the bones of their kneecaps according to Indian rituals. They took care not to trap beavers in the spring so that they could raise their young, and they left a breeding pair in each beaver area so that the population could continue. As once-rich trapping grounds were stripped of their game, Archie began to question his profession. He felt that he was betraying the animals to a common enemy who would soon destroy them all.

In the summer of 1927, Archie sent his aunts a photograph of his young wife. His mother, whom he had not seen since just after the operation on his foot in London, wrote him that his half-brother, Leonard Scott-Brown, wanted to join the Hudson's

# CROSSING THE SLOUGH OF DESPOND

*At one point on the trip to Birch Lake, near Cabano, Quebec, Archie
inadvertently capsized the canoe and all its contents, including two beaver
kittens, who were trapped inside the stove in which they were being
transported. At the time the kittens were suffering from a skin disease
that had rendered them hairless.*

THE CANOE BECAME quickly coated with ice, and the
accumulations that formed on the steel shod pole thickened
it into a club that splashed water at every stroke, so that the
gunnell [sic] was a solid mass of ice and the bottom of the canoe
was like a skating rink. Under these conditions, standing in the
narrow slippery stern, the usual attitude for the sternsman in
poling, was a ticklish business. . . . Putting extra pressure on
the pole in an especially stiff piece of fast
water, my moccasins, frozen and slippery
as glass, shot from under me on the icy canoe
bottom and I fell flat on my face in the river.
I managed to twist clear of the canoe to
avoid upsetting it, but this availed little as
the light craft, out of control, swung side on,
filled, and was forced to the bottom by the
pressure. Anahareo, who was kneeling rolled clear, head first.
Instantly we both regained our feet—swift work to be done, a
matter of seconds! Somewhere under that rushing icy flood,

*Facing page:* The adoption of beaver
kittens McGinnis and McGinty
was the turning point in Archie's life.
He was completely won over by
"their rollicking good fellowship" and
their "child-like intimacies."

perhaps already gone, was the stove and in it the beaver were securely locked without a chance for their lives.

Packs, some air remaining in them momentarily, commenced to float up, and soon the canoe, becoming empty would shift and begin to buckle. We disregarded all this and groped desperately, shoulder deep. Anahareo was swept off her feet once, recovering by some miracle of agility. A beaver suddenly immersed drowns as quickly as any other beast, and we had searched for a full minute. And I think we lost our heads a little for a moment, for suddenly we were holding up the dripping stove between us, although we could never remember the act of finding it, and Anahareo was crying out "They're alive! They're alive!" while I stood stupidly, clutching in my free hand, as though it were a talisman, the handle of our new tea pail, while the pail itself, with the lid on, was bobbing merrily off with our immediate supply of lard, on its way to New Brunswick. The temperature was far below freezing; the water was icy cold and tore at our legs, so that we were like to lose our foothold and be swept away.

The river-bank was some five rods away but Anahareo, by judicious use of her pole, arrived there safely with the stove and its now frantic occupants. Three times she ran the gauntlet of the frigid racing torrent, getting all our stuff ashore, while I, being of longer gear, did the salvaging and raised the canoe. . . .

We had little time for congratulations. It was freezing hard, and ice was forming on everything including our clothes.

We were both soaked to the hide and the beaver in their almost hairless condition were in danger of perishing. Some of the blankets were partly dry, having been in the centre of the bundle, so I wrapped up Anahareo and the beaver together in them, and left them lie there in the snow while I rustled some wood and got an immense fire going, working on the run while the clothes froze on my back. Once the outer clothing is frozen a certain measure of warmth is possible inside them, but I must have resembled a frenziedly active tin-man, and no doubt the whole business, if viewed from a warm safe spot would have been highly entertaining to an onlooker.... Such is life in the woods that what with the great warm fire, a cooking pot half full of tea and a pan full of deer meat, we were again happy and as well off as ever; while the two deep-sea divers sat warm and comfortable on new bedding in their tin hut, eating some candies that were reserved for special occasions and making a great noise about it.

We had lost nothing save the tea pail and a small package of lard, and even two panes of glass tied on to a washboard were recovered intact some distance down stream. My self-esteem, however, had received a severe set-back, for I had committed what, to a canoeman, was in the light of a major crime, which I am here expiating by telling about it from the house-tops.

Inside of a couple of hours we were again on our way, partly dry and as confident as ever, and looked on our mishap as now amounting to little more than a slightly longer dinner hour than we usually allowed ourselves.

Bay Company. Leonard was Kittie's son by her second husband, James Scott-Brown, who had died several years earlier. Leonard came to Canada the following year. After three years with the Hudson's Bay Company, he spent some years trapping in the Northwest Territories before returning to England in 1938. Archie described life on the trapline in his letters to his mother. She found his writing so poetic that she sent copies of his correspondence to the English outdoors magazine *Country Life.* The editors expressed interest in an article on the subject.

Archie had spent the summer fire ranging again. The winter of 1927–28 he and Anahareo were back on the trapline in Quebec. Archie decided to boil a Christmas pudding, a ritual, no doubt, from his childhood. He enlisted Anahareo's help strictly as an assistant, probably out of a sense of self-preservation; he made it clear in his later writings that he thought Anahareo's cooking left much to be desired: "Good old Anahareo! Not much on the skillet, but right there with bells on when work was required to be done." Anahareo once again tried hard to adapt to trapping, but after finding an emaciated lynx that had survived in one of her traps for nearly ten days, she decided that she could no longer bear to kill animals.

In the spring of 1928, Archie and Anahareo found two beaver kittens whose mother had been killed in a trap. Archie's fur catch had been small, and he took the two young beavers home, intending to sell them after they reached town at the end of the trapping season. Anahareo, however, had other ideas; she wanted to keep them as pets.

Archie put the beavers in the metal stove to transport them to town, since this was the only receptacle they had on hand that the beavers could not chew their way out of. The beavers had the run of the campsite at night, and on the journey the two small creatures proceeded to worm their way into Archie's affections. By the time the party reached Doucet, Archie was as attached to the beavers as Anahareo was.

Archie and Anahareo decided to keep the two beaver kittens. They had recently read a book about the construction of the Union Pacific, the first transcontinental railroad in North America. They decided to call the beavers McGinnis and McGinty because their industriousness reminded them of the toils of the Irish construction workers on the rail line.

The summer of 1928, Archie planned to go fire ranging again. But what was he to do for the winter? The prospect of trapping was depressing. His health was not good: he had a weak heart and lungs and a bad foot. Fur-bearing animals were fast disappearing, and Quebec was likely to follow Ontario's lead and ban non-Indian trappers. Anahareo loathed trapping and now they had the baby beavers. But if Archie did not trap, what would they do for money? He had only his meager war pension of $15 a month and the money he earned in the summer as a fire ranger.

In the summer of 1928, Archie announced to Anahareo that he would never hunt beavers again. Henceforth he would work for their preservation. "I am now the President, Treasurer, and sole member of the Society of the Beaver People. How about a donation?" he asked her. He envisioned starting a beaver colony,

60    *Grey Owl*

although he would still have to trap other fur-bearing animals to support the endeavor. The question now was where to start the colony. They needed a place where there were still active beaver lodges and where the beavers would be relatively safe from trappers. Such places were increasingly hard to find.

While Anahareo and Archie were contemplating their next move, they set up camp a mile from the town of Senneterre. One day when Archie was in town collecting mail and supplies, the Macs decided they were not enjoying it in the stove and they started to complain. Anahareo was offering them reassurance through the stovepipe hole when a tall, elderly Indian walked into camp and asked her what she was doing. The Indian's name was Dave White Stone, and one of his great loves was prospecting, an interest Anahareo shared. Anahareo explained about the beavers, and Dave came to live with Archie and Anahareo for a while. He stayed until Archie and Anahareo decided to leave for a land they had heard still abounded in game. Archie, Anahareo, and the two Macs took the train to Cabano, Quebec, in Témiscouata County, close to the New Brunswick border. They could not afford the fare for Dave and promised to send for him as soon as they were able.

Cabano was a sorry disappointment, as the area had been heavily logged. Archie and Anahareo decided they had little choice but to stay, and they set up camp for the winter of 1928–29

*Facing page:* Archie's first public appearance was with Jelly Roll in the resort town of Métis, Quebec, in the summer of 1929. Presenting himself as the half-breed conservationist Archie Belaney, he raised $700 towards his proposed beaver colony.

# $\mathcal{A}$ MEMORABLE CHRISTMAS

*In later years, Archie wrote fondly of the Christmas he and Anahareo spent with the two Macs in the cabin at Birch Lake. The two Macs had constructed a sleeping chamber behind a barricade underneath one of the bunks in the cabin where they could retire when they felt in need of privacy.*

ON CHRISTMAS EVE all was ready. But there was one thing missing; Anahareo decided that the beavers were to have a Christmas Tree. So while I lit the lantern and arranged the candles so their light fell on the decorations to best advantage, and put apples and oranges and nuts in dishes on the table, and tended the saddle of deer meat that sizzled alongside of the factory-made Christmas pudding that was boiling on top of the little stove, Anahareo took axe and snowshoes and went into the starry Christmas night. . . .

*Facing page: The beaver kittens Archie and Anahareo adopted filled their lives with delight. They were constantly amazed by the beavers' industrious and enterprising natures.*

Anahareo had got a fine balsam fir, a very picture of a Christmas tree, which she wedged upright in a crevice in the floor poles. On top of it she put a lighted candle, and on the limbs tied candies, and pieces of apple. . . .

The beaver viewed these preparations with no particular enthusiasm but before long, attracted by the odour of the tree, they found the hanging tidbits and sampled them, and soon were busy cutting the strings and pulling them down and eating them with great gusto. . . . They soon consumed all there was on the

tree, and as these were replaced the now thoroughly aroused little creatures stood up on their hind legs and grabbed and pulled at their presents, and stole choice morsels from one another, pushing and shoving so that one would sometimes fall and scramble to his feet again as hastily as possible, for fear every-thing would be gone before he got up, while they screeched and chattered and squealed in their excitement. And we forgot our supper, and laughed and called out at them, and they would run to us excitedly and back to the tree with little squawks as if to say "Looky! what we found!" And when they could eat no more they commenced to carry away provision against the morrow, sometimes between their teeth, on all fours, or staggering along erect with some prized tidbit clutched tightly in their arms, each apparently bent on getting all that could be got while it lasted. And when we thought they had enough and no longer made replacements, McGinty, the wise and the thrifty, pulled down the tree and started away with it, as though she figured on another crop appearing later and had decided to corner the source of the supply. . . .

*Facing page:* The House of McGinnis was an isolated cabin on Birch Lake in Quebec. Here Archie and Anahareo passed some of the happiest months of their time together.

Stuffed to the ears, and having a goodly supply cached behind the barricade, the revellers, tired now, or perhaps overcome by a pleasant fullness, soon went behind it too. Heavy sighs and mumbles of contentment came up from the hidden chamber beneath the bunk and soon, surrounded by all the Christmas Cheer they had collected, they fell asleep.

at Birch Lake. It was an arduous journey to the lake by canoe—at one point they upset the complete contents of the boat into the river—followed by a dreadful six-mile portage in to the lake, but finally a cabin was constructed that would one day be known as the House of McGinnis. They did find a beaver house on the lake but there was little game in the area on which to support themselves. Archie worried that he might have to kill the beavers and sell their skins if he and Anahareo were to survive the winter. He had to find another way to bring in some money.

Archie and Anahareo whiled away the long hours in the cabin at Birch Lake exchanging stories and reading books and magazines. Archie wrote a long rebuttal to a magazine article on ridding Algonquin Park in Ontario of wolves by dropping strychnine pellets from airplanes. He also responded to a request of the editors of *Country Life* and wrote an article on life in the bush. When he snowshoed to town to get supplies for a Christmas celebration, he made a trip to the post office to collect his monthly pension checks and to entrust his writings to the mail. Apart from planning Christmas surprises for each other and for the beavers, Archie and Anahareo spent the winter months planning their beaver colony.

It was March before Archie made it into town again. Anahareo went with him. This time when he visited the post office to pick up his pension checks, there was a package waiting for him. It was a copy of the latest edition of *Country Life* and a check for his article. Here at last was what he had been looking for: a way of making money to support his beaver colony. Not only that, but the editors at *Country Life* had been so pleased with the article that they had included a request for a book on the subject. The article had inadvertently been published under Archie's mother's name, since she had been the one to submit it, but no matter, that oversight could easily be corrected. Archie and Anahareo were ecstatic. They hurried back to the cabin with their heads full of plans for the future.

When Archie and Anahareo got back to Birch Lake they found that Dave White Stone had arrived in their absence. Being a trapper and knowing that Archie was also a trapper, he had killed the family of beavers in the lodge on the lake and had the skins waiting as a welcome-home surprise for them. Archie and Anahareo were devastated. With the beavers gone from Birch Lake, they had little hope of starting a beaver colony there. They decided to move the two Macs to Lake Touladi between Squatteck and Cabano and try their luck there. On their arrival at Touladi, as Archie and Anahareo were setting up camp, the two Macs disappeared. Archie and Anahareo, aided by Dave, searched fruitlessly. Archie wandered so far in search of them that his wounded foot began to give him trouble and he could not walk on it for weeks. In the end, they decided the young beavers had likely fallen victim to a local trapper. Their fortunes were at a low ebb.

Dave saw how upset Archie and Anahareo were, and he found two beaver kittens to replace the two Macs. Only one survived; she was christened Jelly Roll. Archie and Anahareo then moved from their tent camp at Lake Touladi to an abandoned

logger's cabin on Hay Lake, not far from Cabano. Once they were settled, Archie began to work on the manuscript for *Country Life*. Since Archie was not good company when he was writing, Anahareo decided to spend the summer looking for minerals in the North. Perhaps she would strike it rich and their financial worries would be over.

When Anahareo returned at the end of the summer in 1929, she and Archie set off with Jelly Roll for Métis, a fashionable seaside resort on the St. Lawrence River, northeast of Cabano, where Archie hoped to make money as a guide. Unfortunately, there were no jobs for guides, and Archie had to settle for being a gardener's assistant and charging the curious 10 cents apiece to view Jelly Roll. Meanwhile, Anahareo let people know about Archie's article in *Country Life* and their plans to start a beaver colony. Mrs. Madeline Peck, a summer resident from Montreal, was impressed with the manuscript-in-progress that Anahareo showed her and arranged for Archie to give a talk at the Seaside Hotel on the conservation of wildlife.

Archie was very nervous about the talk. He said later that he "felt a good deal like a snake that has swallowed an icicle, chilled from one end to the other." Despite Archie's apprehension, the talk was a great success and earned them $700 in donations towards their beaver colony. Archie was asked to give other lectures and to address a Boy Scout troop on bush craft. When he and

*Facing page:* By the fall of 1929, Archie was getting a reputation as "the beaver man" and was visited by the media; this photograph was taken at his cabin near Cabano in November 1929. The following year he used the name Grey Owl for this first time.

Anahareo returned with Jelly Roll to the cabin on Hay Lake, they had over $1,000 in their pockets. The talk in Métis marked the beginning of Archie's career as a public personality.

News of Archie and his beaver began to travel, and in November a French-Canadian journalist from Quebec City, Jean-Charles Harvey, paid Archie and Anahareo a visit. Archie was still advertising his "half-breed" origins, and Harvey seemed to be taken in by Archie's Indian image. Archie must have found this public recognition of his private fantasy gratifying. Up until now, he had told stories about his origins only to people he knew. This was his first chance to see how convincing these stories would be to those who did not know him. The outside world, it seemed, was happy to take him at his word.

That winter, Anahareo left again, this time with Dave on the trail of a gold mine in northern Quebec. Archie stayed behind with Jelly Roll for company, working on the manuscript for *Country Life*. During the long, lonely winter he turned to Jelly Roll for companionship and for a second opinion on his writing:

> When she was on the bunk with me she would reach out very often at my note book and other papers, and we sometimes had lively discussions on this matter in which I was not always the winner.... [Jelly] had registered her entire approval of my literary efforts by removing the ms. bodily. A few sheets of my work were scattered on the floor, but the rest were not to be seen. A visit of investigation to the abode of the culprit was

received with squeals of mingled trepidation and protest, but I routed her out and raked up the manuscript with the blackened wooden poker and a piece of wire, the paper fiend meanwhile trying desperately to maintain her rights of ownership.

Since Archie had not numbered the pages, it took considerable time and effort to reconstruct the manuscript. Despite the trouble Jelly caused him, however, he was infinitely patient with her. He slept on the floor because she could not reach him when he was in his bunk, he let her use his sleeping blankets as towels to dry off with after a swim, and he ungrudgingly repaired the household items she would inevitably gnaw on. Perhaps he was providing his beaver with the indulgence he had so longed for and Aunt Ada had been so loath to give when he was a child.

Over the past year, Archie had submitted a number of articles to the editor of *Canadian Forest and Outdoors*. The editor had contacted the Parks Branch, since he thought the federal department might be interested in Archie's conservationist message. The system of national parks had been set up across Canada in 1885, and the Parks Branch was looking for ways of raising its profile with the public. Archie, or "the beaver man," as he was coming to be known, might be just what the department was looking for. In the spring of 1930, Archie received a visit from the Parks Branch publicity director, J. C. Campbell, who wanted to investigate the possibility of shooting a film of Archie and his beaver to make "a living argument for conservation."

# JELLY ROLL

*When Archie wrote he needed to be alone. Anahareo responded by pursuing her own interests in prospecting in the North. Having driven Anahareo away, Archie turned to Jelly Roll for companionship.*

IN THIS CREATURE there was life and understanding; she moved and talked and did things, and gave me a response of which I had not thought an animal capable. She seemed to supply some need in my life of which I had been only dimly conscious heretofore, which had been growing with the years, and which marriage had for a time provided....

This creature comported itself as a person, of a kind, and she busied herself at tasks that I could, without loss of dignity, have occupied myself at: she made camp, procured and carried in supplies, could lay plans and carry them out and stood robustly and resolutely on her own hind legs, metaphorically and actually, and had an independence of spirit that measured up well with my own, seeming to look on me as a contemporary, accepting me as an equal and no more. I could in no way see where I was the loser from this association, and would not, if I could, have asserted my superiority, save as was sometimes necessary to avert wilful destruction.

Any branches brought in for feed ... were ... neatly piled near the water supply, nor would she suffer any sticks or loose

*Facing page: Jelly Roll starred in the five beaver films shot by the National Parks Board of Canada.*

materials to be scattered on the floor; these she always removed
and relegated to a junk pile she kept under one of the windows.
This I found applied to socks, moccasins, the wash board and the
broom, etc., as well as to sticks. This broom was to her a kind
of staff of office which she, as self-appointed janitor, was forever
carrying around with her on her tours of
inspection, and it also served, when turned end
for end, as a quick, if rather dry lunch. . . .
She would delicately snip the straws off it, one
at a time, and holding them with one end in her
mouth would push them slowly in, while the
teeth, working at great speed, chopped it into
tiny portions. This operation resembled the
performance of a sword swallower as much as it
did anything else, and the sound produced was
similar to that of a sewing machine running a little out of control.
A considerable dispute raged over this broom, but in the end I
found it easier to buy new brooms and keep my mouth shut.

*Facing page:* Jelly Roll learned to
open the lower half of the cabin door,
which she did with characteristic
vigor. Archie wrote that there were
occasions when Jelly Roll had "the
same air of disapproval one detects in
the presence of a landlady with whom
one is a little behind with the rent."

Her attempts at communication with me, sometimes ludicrous,
often pitiful, and frequently quite understandable, as I got to
know them, placed her, to my mind, high above the plane
of ordinary beasts. This, and the community of interest we had
of keeping things in shape, of keeping up the home so to speak,
strengthened indissolubly the bond between the two of us,
both creatures that were never meant to live alone.

In June 1930, Archie had his first article published in *Canadian Forest and Outdoors*; over the next twelve months, at least nine more were to appear. Earlier that year Archie had set a trap for a marauding otter but had caught a young beaver instead. Archie had nursed the injured beaver back to health and had christened him Rawhide. Together with Jelly Roll, he appeared in the film *Beaver People* shot by the National Parks Branch in Cabano that summer.

Anahareo returned at the end of the summer to find Archie still hard at work on the manuscript for *Country Life*. Exasperated, she left again, this time for the exclusive Seigneury Club at Montebello, on the Ottawa River between Ottawa and Montreal, where she was to drive dog teams for tourists taking a winter break.

In mid-November a solitary Archie was writing and drinking in the cabin at Hay Lake when he received an invitation to address the annual convention of the Canadian Forestry Association in Montreal, where the beaver film was to be shown for the first time. This was momentous news. Although Archie had little experience lecturing, he realized that the medium was as important as the message. He had already been described in the media as a reformed halfbreed trapper, but this grand occasion seemed to call for a more dramatic image. His transformation into the Indian conservationist Grey Owl had begun. He tried out the new name in a letter to his editors at *Country Life*, and the response must have encouraged him to forge ahead with his plan.

*Facing page:* The newly minted Grey Owl found his niche as a spokesperson for Canada's national parks. In 1931 he and his beavers moved to a cabin the Parks Branch had constructed for him at Beaver Lodge Lake in Riding Mountain National Park, Manitoba.

Archie was nervous about his public debut as Grey Owl and needed moral support. In late January, Anahareo received a cryptic message from her husband asking her to travel to the Windsor Hotel at once and to ask for Grey Owl. Intrigued, she came on January 23, in time to attend her husband's maiden speech in his new persona. The event was a huge success. It set the pattern for numerous speeches Grey Owl was to give, dressed in his Indian regalia, with films of his tame beaver to illustrate his stories.

*Facing page:* After six months at Riding Mountain, Grey Owl and his beavers settled in Prince Albert National Park, Saskatchewan. The cabin and the beaver lodge were built so that the beaver lodge opened up into the interior of the cabin.

In his dramatic public presentations as Grey Owl, Archie portrayed Anahareo as the woman by his side. In reality, what he gained in fame, he lost in his personal life. From the time his public mission was assured, Archie spent most of the rest of his life without the woman who had helped him find it. As he continued to immerse himself in writing books and articles, she continued to create a life of her own. They would never recapture the magic of that winter at Birch Lake when Anahareo and the two Macs were the center of Archie's universe: "Far below I could see the tiny glow of the lighted tent that sheltered all I cared for in the world, a weary waiting woman, and two small orphaned creatures." This was the time when they had shared their life stories and laid their plans for the beaver colony. But it was no longer just the two of them in a remote cabin with their beavers. As Archie embraced a wider audience, he found himself losing his connection with the woman who used to be the one who listened to all his stories.

Apart from his increasing estrangement from Anahareo, Grey Owl's other problem in the spring of 1931 was with his beavers. Jelly Roll and Rawhide had holed up in their own lodge for the winter, and Grey Owl had no idea how they would behave come spring. This was the first winter Jelly had not spent with him, and Archie was worried about whether she would return to him, or whether the less domesticated Rawhide would persuade her to try her luck in the wild. In an article published in *Canadian Forest and Outdoors* in March 1931 he went so far as to suggest that the beavers had been killed—just in case they decided not to return.

While Grey Owl fretted over his beavers, the Parks Branch was realizing that he could be a powerful spokesperson for its cause. In early 1931 the branch offered him a post as caretaker of park animals at Riding Mountain National Park in Manitoba. He was employed under the name of Archie Belaney, but henceforth he was known to the public as Grey Owl. In the article published in March 1931 in *Canadian Forest and Outdoors*, there was an autobiographical essay by the new celebrity, outlining his Indian heritage. In honor of the recognition his new role had received, Archie appended an Ojibway translation to his name: the author of the article was cited as Grey Owl, or Wa-sha-quon-asin, He Who Walks By Night.

To Grey Owl's enormous relief, both Jelly Roll and Rawhide reappeared in the spring of 1931. The Parks Branch had built a brand-new cabin for Grey Owl, Anahareo, and the beavers at

Beaver Lodge Lake in Riding Mountain National Park. A special tank was constructed to transport the beavers from Quebec, and Anahareo accompanied the group as far as Toronto before setting out on a brief prospecting trip.

Events did not turn out as planned, however, for either Anahareo or the beavers. Water levels on the prairies were perilously low in the early 1930s, and the lake at Riding Mountain was too shallow to provide the beavers with adequate protection over the winter. As for Anahareo, her camp fell victim to fire. She traveled to Riding Mountain to look after the beavers while Grey Owl scouted out a more suitable location for them in the newly created Prince Albert National Park in the neighboring province of Saskatchewan.

Grey Owl found what he considered the perfect location: Lake Ajawaan, thirty miles from the summer tent town of Waskesiu:

> Ajawaan; a small, deep lake that, like a splash of quicksilver, lies gleaming in its setting of the wooded hills that stretch in long, heaving undulations into the North, to the Arctic Sea. Its waters by day reflect its countless moods, and the ever-changing colours of the sky; today a perfect shadowgraph of the surrounding woods, unruffled, lucent and jade green; to-night, silver in a flood of moonlight, and at the end of every day, crimson with the glory of the sunset.

Here a cabin was to be built to Grey Owl's specifications to accommodate the conservationist and his beavers. The cabin was designed to allow the construction of a beaver dam half in and half out of the cabin. In this way, Grey Owl would be able to keep a constant eye on his charges.

In the meantime, in June 1931 Parks Branch cameraman Bill Oliver arrived at Riding Mountain to make a second beaver film, and late in 1931 Grey Owl's first book, *The Men of the Last Frontier*, was published in England by *Country Life*. The publishing experience had not been a happy one for Grey Owl, for he had not taken kindly to having his work edited. Because he wanted to give the impression that he was a bush Indian rather than an educated Englishman, he wished to retain idiosyncratic spelling and infelicities of grammar. He was so distressed about the editing—and about the fact that the title had been changed from *The Vanishing Frontier* to *The Men of the Last Frontier* without his consent—that he sought out a new British publisher for his later works. On the advice of his publisher in Canada, Hugh Eayrs at Macmillan, he chose Lovat Dickson, a Canadian who had recently started his own publishing house in London.

*Facing page:* Grey Owl and Anahareo executed their duties as ambassadors for the park by entertaining tourists at Beaver Lodge. Dignitaries who came to visit included Canadian prime-minister-to-be John Diefenbaker and the governor-general of Canada, Lord Tweedsmuir.

In October 1931, Grey Owl, Anahareo, Jelly Roll, Rawhide, and beaver kittens Wakanee, Wakanoo, Silver Bells, and Buckshot moved from Riding Mountain to Prince Albert National Park. Grey Owl had probably been surprised by the appearance of the kittens, for when Jelly Roll had gone into hibernation the previous

winter, he had thought she was a male. The mistake was soon corrected, and in the books he wrote about his beavers he always referred to Jelly as a female.

When the party arrived at Beaver Lodge in early November, the beavers were kept in captivity until the lake froze over. Had the beavers been left to their own devices, they might have gone out onto the lake to gather sticks to build a lodge despite the lateness of the season. As beavers work at night, while they were out busily collecting suitable building materials, the entrance to the lodge might have frozen over with ice too thick for them to break through. Denied entrance to their winter home, they would quickly have frozen to death. Confined to the cabin as they were, they were unable to forage for food. To ensure that they had enough to eat to last them through the winter, Grey Owl got a feed raft together and anchored it just outside the cabin.

Grey Owl's official duties at the park were to observe the beavers and to record their activity. He found the change from life on the trail to a sedentary life unsettling and worried that he might lose the skills in which he had previously taken so much pride. As he had so often done before, however, he applied himself single-mindedly to the task at hand and devoted himself to the study of his beavers. Grey Owl did not see himself as a naturalist whose job it was to take measurements and make scientific observations. To him, each animal was an individual with its own distinct character, and this was the aspect of animal behavior that he wished to record.

For the Parks Branch, Grey Owl was an ambassador who spread the message of conservation to those who came to visit the cabin on Lake Ajawaan. And people traveled from around the world to see him. Grey Owl and Anahareo, when she was there, entertained their visitors graciously, showing off the beavers and explaining their habits and dispositions. A Dutch tourist recorded the following observation:

> We are lucky, Grey Owl is home.... A tall, lithe figure, in buckskin pants and a red shirt, his long hair parted in two braids. He greets us in the way of the Redman—his hand held above his brow—and helps us disembark from our canoe. A squirrel climbs up his leg, snatching a peanut from his fingers, while a jay circles around him begging for a piece of bread.

In December 1931, much to her astonishment, Anahareo became pregnant. She had long given up on the idea of having children and had devoted herself to the beaver family and prospecting instead. That winter she did not travel but stayed within the confines of Beaver Lodge. In January 1932, Grey Owl started on his second book-length manuscript, *Pilgrims of the Wild*. The beavers, who had been imprisoned before freeze-up, now began constructing a lodge half in, half out of the cabin, using peeled poplar sticks from the feed raft. The lodge progressed at the rate the beaver family ate the bark off the sticks. What with Archie's demands for peace and quiet and the beavers' constant activity at night,

# THE ANIMALS OF AJAWAAN

*Grey Owl's cabin in Prince Albert National Park was thirty miles from the nearest human settlement. It was, however, situated in the middle of a busy and varied animal community. Visitors to the lodge saw not only Grey Owl's famous beavers, but also the birds, squirrels, and moose that frequently came to visit.*

GREY OWL ENJOYED *the company of the mischievous whiskey jack.* This whiskey-jack is a small bird, about the size of a blackbird, but he has more mischief in his small body than there is in a whole bag of cats. He is a scamp, but a likeable rascal at that. He mocks the calls of other birds and steals bait, or any small articles left around the camp. He loves human company, and, at the first smoke of a camp-fire, he appears mysteriously from nowhere, like a small grey shadow, and perches on a limb. . . . A man alone for months is glad of their company, in spite of the trouble they make; and for me their friendliness and cheerful whistling have brightened many a lonesome camp fire. *Hummingbirds were like little jewels flying through the forest.* The most resplendent of all my bird guests is a hum-ming bird. He is a tiny, lustrous little creature, and his feathers are so very miniature that they seem like tiny scales, and in his tightly-fitting, iridescent sheath of opal, emerald and ruby

*Facing page: The whiskey jacks at Ajawaan would descend on Grey Owl looking for food whenever he came out of the cabin. He appreciated their lively company and mischievous temperaments.*

red, he seems more like some priceless, delicate work of Chinese artistry, than a living thing. For a short time only he stays, hovering among the wild rose bushes, his wings winnowing at an incredible speed, so as to be a nearly invisible blurr [sic] until he darts away with almost bullet-like velocity, a brilliant streak of fabulous coloration.

*Facing page:* Grey Owl bottle-feeds young twin moose. Over the years he also developed a relationship with a bull moose he named Charlie, who was quite tame except in the rutting season. He often came and stood by the cabin door, much to the consternation of the beavers.

*Bears were a common sight in the area, and they generally were not a problem if they were left to their own devices.* It is no uncommon thing to meet a bear or so walking peacefully along the highway. The streets of the tent city [Waskesiu] are lighted up at night, but the lights are some distance apart, and it has been suggested that more lights be provided so the bears can see their way around and not get scared stiff by having people bump into them at night.

*Grey Owl was less accommodating of predatory animals, such as wolves.* After a while the sound of the fire died away, and I had lost track of things until I suddenly awoke chilled clear through, to find the fire low, and the echo of some sound dying away across the empty hills.

I listened for a while, and almost dozed again, when the sound was repeated; long, drawn out, and distant, mournful as the cry of a lost soul. The echoes didn't have time to fade away before it was answered from some place on the lake, right close to camp. Wolves! . . .

*About a week later, Grey Owl encountered the wolves out on the ice and shot a few of them.* Pride forbids me to say how few wolves I killed that night, considering the amount of ammunition I used, but at forty dollars each as the bounty then was, I was able to buy me some long needed renewals in my outfit, and have some left over.

*One of Grey Owl's companions at Ajawaan was a pet moose called Charlie.* As I was making my preparations [to leave for Waskesiu] I heard, outside, a sort of light crackling, crushing sound, and looking through the window saw my friend the moose . . . walking slowly, steadily, and very thoroughly, through and along my canoe. I rushed out of the cabin at him, shouting, and this seemed to remind him of something, so he extricated his feet from the various holes, where they must have felt most uncomfortable, and stood aside, surveying the wreckage with an air of rather thoughtful detachment. Now this was nothing but rank carelessness on his part, and I remember having a distinct feeling of annoyance about it. Granted that he was a youngish moose, and perhaps didn't know very much, the fact still remains that a canoe is a very handy thing to have when you have a thirty mile trip to make, entirely by water.

*Jelly, however, was always his favorite.* She lies there with her head on my knee as in the old days, making soft murmuring noises in her dozing, she is no more Queen of the Beaver People,

*Facing page:* Because beavers are nocturnal, and because Jelly Roll and the other beavers could enter the cabin at any time, Grey Owl took to writing at night and sleeping during the day. He often spent more time with the beavers than he did with his human companions.

but is just Jelly the old-timer-the Tub. If I move she will clutch at my clothing to keep me there, and make sounds I hear from her at no other time. And then her voice is like a muted keyboard that runs the gamut of her emotions, recording every slightest variation; or like some delicately balanced instrument on which impressions come and go, swiftly wavering back and forth, even as her rich, dark fur mirrors the gossamer touch of every imperceptible, tiny breeze that stirs it ever and anon. And when I look down at the ugly body, unlovely till you see the eyes, I cannot but think that beauty may not be all in form, but may rest in strength, in grace of motion, in symmetry and rhythm, and in fidelity, and in a harmonious conformation to an environment.

it must have been anything but a restful winter for Anahareo. She retaliated by taking a correspondence course in mineralogy.

In the winter the cabin door had been cut in two since beavers have the habit of filling every air-spilling crack they can find and were forever putting mud seals as far as they could reach up around the door frame. Rather than destroy their work each time he wanted to go in or out of the cabin—to say nothing of encountering Jelly's wrath at his meddlesome ways—Grey Owl decided to saw the door in two and just step over the bottom half. When summer came, Jelly Roll learned to open the bottom portion of the door for herself, from both inside and out. With the cabin door constantly swinging open as the beavers went about their business, Grey Owl and Anahareo soon gave up trying to keep the flies out.

Near her due date, Anahareo traveled down to Prince Albert, and on August 23, 1932, Dawn was born. When Anahareo traveled back up to Ajawaan with her baby daughter, she found, to her horror, the roof off the cabin and the beavers traipsing purposefully across the living room floor clutching short armfuls of mud. Grey Owl was in the middle of orchestrating yet another beaver film with Bill Oliver, who was perched on the frame of the cabin where the roof should have been recording the beavers' solemn progress from above. Grey Owl was excited about the publicity the film would bring to his beaver program; Anahareo retreated to the upper cabin that had been built to accommodate her on her return with the baby.

*Facing page:* In the fall of 1932 Dawn was born at the hospital in Prince Albert. Grey Owl had a second cabin built for Anahareo and Dawn behind Beaver Lodge. In later years this cabin was used for visitors.

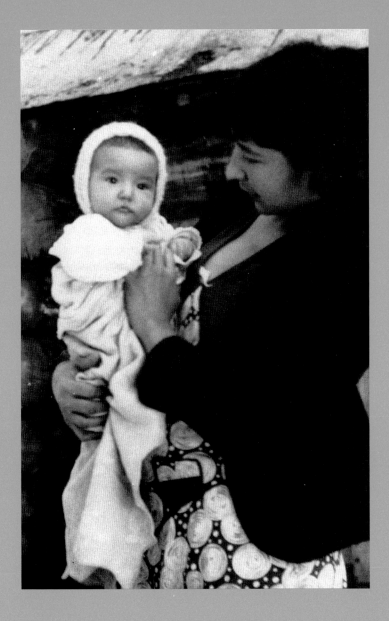

Anahareo and Dawn spent the winter of 1932 with Grey Owl at Beaver Lodge. They mostly stayed in the upper cabin, since the beavers were active at night and Grey Owl did not like to be disturbed when he was writing. In March 1933 Anahareo could stand the isolation no longer. She took Dawn to stay with the Winters family in Prince Albert and in May she left for a brief prospecting trip. One of the local game wardens had recommended Mrs. Winters, a respected individual in the community, as someone who might teach Anahareo how to care for a new baby. As it turned out, Mrs. Winters became a surrogate mother for Dawn, who was often left with the Winters family when Anahareo went prospecting and Archie was holed up in his remote cabin writing. On Anahareo's return in 1933, she and Dawn spent the summer at Beaver Lodge and the following winter with the Winterses. In 1934 Anahareo left for another prospecting trip, and this time she stayed away for over a year.

In April 1935, during Anahareo's extended absence, Grey Owl received a note from a book critic in Toronto to say that he had heard a rumor from an acquaintance of Grey Owl's that he was not the Indian he pretended to be and that he had "assumed the Red Brother for artistic effect." Grey Owl was panic-stricken. After firing off a quick rebuttal, he went to Prince Albert to soothe his nerves with three weeks of heavy drinking.

In August 1935 Grey Owl wrote to Anahareo telling her he was about to go on a tour of Britain and asking her to come home. His second book, *Pilgrims of the Wild*, had been published to critical acclaim the previous year by Hugh Eayrs at Macmillan in Canada, Lovat Dickson in Great Britain, and Maxwell Perkins at Scribner's in the United States. Lovat Dickson wanted Grey Owl to tour Britain to promote both *Pilgrims* and *The Adventures of Sajo and Her Beaver People*, a children's book Dickson had commissioned that was due to come out in the fall of 1935. Anahareo caught a train back to Prince Albert, spent a week with Dawn in town, and then went to Ajawaan to look after the beavers for the five months that Grey Owl was to be away.

By the time Grey Owl left on his first British lecture tour, his often stormy relationship with Anahareo was drawing to a close. Anahareo had never allowed Grey Owl's strong personality to overwhelm her, and that had resulted in many altercations over the years. One story from Ajawaan tells of a drunken Anahareo taking potshots at the heels of an equally drunken Grey Owl as he ran from tree to tree outside the cabin. When Anahareo had left for her extended absence in 1934, she had departed without telling Grey Owl of her plans and had decided that she would not return to Beaver Lodge unless Grey Owl expressly invited her to. He was as stubborn as she was, and he did not extend an invitation until he had to call her home to look after the beavers. Although he was to introduce her to audiences in Britain as the star of his show, by the time he got to England the images he presented were all that remained of the relationship that they had once had.

*Facing page:* Grey Owl's writings soon garnered him an international reputation and his British publisher arranged a publicity tour for him. Grey Owl wanted to present himself not as a former half-breed trapper but as an Indian chief, and he prepared accordingly.

PART THREE

# A Message for the World

IN PREPARATION for his trip to Britain, Grey Owl flew to La Ronge in northern Saskatchewan. Just as he had known how crucial appearance was for his debut as Grey Owl in Montreal, he knew that the image he presented to the British public was going to be of the utmost importance. Grey Owl bought five moose hides and two pounds of beads for Anahareo to use in sewing him an outfit. She had three weeks to complete the work. He was determined that people were going to get their money's worth and were going to see the North

American Indian they expected to see. Judging from the accolades he garnered, his presentation found its mark: "Gray Owl [sic] steps right out of the pages of James Fenimore Cooper. He looks too good to be true to life. With his marvelous, sculptured face; his great feather and fringed buckskin costume; his long, lean body and powerful shoulders. He moves with the grace of a cat; or sits motionless as a perched eagle; yet he is absolutely without pose."

To those who found his presentation overdone, and who perhaps wondered if he was the person he claimed to be, his powerful oration and sincere delivery overcame all doubts. Even though the dramatic persona of a North American Indian may have been what first drew the crowds, what held them were the powerful stories this Indian told. Geoffrey Turner was an ethnologist who had his doubts about Grey Owl's authenticity. He became suspicious when the so-called Indian began his presentation at Oxford City Hall with a Sioux greeting—*How Kola*—an expression that was used by neither the Ojibway nor the Apache to whom Grey Owl claimed allegiance. Turner's doubts, however, were overcome, or at least ceased to be a concern, as soon as Grey Owl delivered the heart of his conservationist message: "My heart sank. But as he got going the Hiawatha stuff vanished and we got down to the real Grey Owl—a man of acute perception, poetic feeling and whimsical humor, and an ardent faith in his mission of wild life conservation ... fascinating."

*Facing page:* Grey Owl had Anahareo sew him an elaborately beaded costume decorated with a beaver and a Canadian maple leaf. He bade farewell to Dawn and set off to deliver his message to the world.

Archie Belaney had always enjoyed being different. He had always enjoyed spinning tales and holding audiences in his thrall. He had used deception to hone his skills, but now, as Grey Owl, he moved beyond tall tales about his personal history to offer perceptive insights into people's relationships with animals and the rest of nature. He found he could speak to issues that he cared about deeply—and people would listen.

Grey Owl's message was one of respect for all people, no matter what their station in life, respect for animals as cohabitants in nature and not as commodities for people to exploit, and respect for nature in itself, a resource to which people could do irremediable harm. He understood the need for people to hunt and to harvest natural resources. He just asked that these activities be undertaken in a responsible and respectful manner. This was the message he brought with him from Canada to the audiences of Britain.

Audiences in Britain listened because Grey Owl's appearance commanded attention and conformed with their expectations—even though he had come from afar, there was an element of the familiar in him. They listened because they believed that as a North American Indian, he was an authority on his subject. They listened because he was charismatic and had a flair for the dramatic—his films and writings about the beavers were powerful illustrations of the changes in attitude he was advocating. They listened because he sincerely believed in his message and did not seem to want personal gain. They also listened because what he was saying struck a chord in a country dealing with the industrial crisis brought on by the Great Depression, with the knowledge of the destruction that could be wrought by war, and with fears for what the future might hold:

> [Grey Owl] made pure Canada, the Canada outside the concrete urban enclosures come alive.... Suddenly here was this romantic figure telling them with his deep and thrilling voice that somewhere there was a land where life could begin again, a place which the screams of demented dictators could not reach, where the air was fresh and not stagnant with the fumes of industry, where wild animals and men could co-exist without murderous intent. It was threatened by the same forces that had overwhelmed them, but there were places like Ajawaan where there was peace.

On tour, Grey Owl showed the same single-mindedness he had shown in his other endeavors. In four months, from October 28, 1935, to February 8, 1936, he spoke to over half a million people and attended over two hundred meetings. He gave up to four lectures a day, and some venues attracted audiences of two to three thousand people. In addition to the tour commitments, he spoke at a literary luncheon at a noted London bookstore and gave a national radio broadcast on the British Broadcasting Corporation.

For the time he was based in London, Grey Owl invited himself to stay in Lovat Dickson's home rather than in a hotel. There he drank, played the gramophone way too loud, and generally had

# On North American Indians

*In an age when few spoke out about their Indian heritage, Grey Owl went out of his way to embrace a culture to which he belonged only in spirit. He believed Indians were the perfect choice for guardians of what was left of the Canadian wilderness, and he was not afraid to broadcast his message wherever he traveled. He was partly responsible for the image, popular today, of Indians as natural conservationists.*

INDIANS ARE IN TUNE with their surroundings, and that accounts to a large extent for their ability in the old days to detect the foreign element in the atmosphere of the woods and plains. A movement where all should be still; a disturbance of the colour scheme; a disarrangement in the set of the leaves; the frayed edge of a newly-broken stick, speak loud to the Indian's eye. They have catalogued and docketed every possible combination of shape, sound, and colour possible in their surroundings, and any deviation from these, however slight, at once strikes a dissonance, as a false note in an orchestra of many instruments is plain to the ear of a musician. . . .

A change of wind they forecast quite accurately and even if sleeping the changed atmospheric conditions brought about by its turning from the South to the North awaken the older people, and they will say, "It is Keewaydin; the North Wind is blowing."

We must not fail to remember that we are still our brother's keeper, and having carelessly allowed this same brother to be robbed of his rights and very means of existence (solemnly agreed by treaty to be inalienable and perpetual, whereby he was a self-supporting producer, a contributor to the wealth of the country and an unofficial game warden and conservationist whose knowledge of wild life would have been invaluable) we must now support him. And this will complete his downfall by the degrading 'dole' system.

The Indian is not to be an object of pity and charity, but ought to be self-supporting, and has a very real, and very useful place to fulfill in the economic life of Canada.

My suggestion...was that that place lay in work connected with the administering, protection and proper control of our natural resources, particularly in relation to wild life, timber and allied issues; at these the Indian is expert and his technical knowledge, accumulated during thousands of years of study and observation, could be of immense value in helping to save from destruction Canada's wilderness country and its inhabitants, which are, together, Canada's greatest asset, and are suffering great loss from the lack of proper knowledge displayed by many of those who are trying to handle them.

to be looked after. Lovat Dickson wrote: "I have a very deep affection for him and regard him as a genius but with some of the characteristics of a small child." The strain of staying so close to the place where he had grown up must have been enormous. He stuck to his story of his Scottish father and Indian mother and his childhood spent on the banks of the Rio Grande. Lovat Dickson accepted it completely.

*Facing page:* In 1935–36 Grey Owl toured Britain for four solid months from Scotland to the south coast. The British public, weary from the Depression, flocked to hear him speak about the clean air and wide open spaces of the Canadian North.

At the end of the tour Betty Somervell, who had acted as his chauffeur during the latter part of the tour, offered to accompany him on the ocean liner back to Canada. She was well aware that there was more to the "modern Hiawatha" than met the public eye and had been warned that the exhausted Grey Owl would likely turn to drink. Despite her constant vigilance on the ocean voyage, he managed to smuggle bottles of whiskey into his cabin. When Betty Somervell finally put a stop to his drinking, Grey Owl found an irrepressible urge to talk and he dictated to her, at great speed, sections of a new book, *Tales of an Empty Cabin.* Once on the train, Grey Owl continued to be unpredictable and demanding. After an overnight stop in Montreal, Betty Somervell wrote in her diary: "In G.O.'s room the telephone was broken. At 7:30 a wild figure with flying hair appeared at my door, in despair because no one would wake him up with tea." One of Grey Owl's prized possessions on that journey was an elaborate Plains Indian headdress constructed in Britain. He babied it all the way home in the train, fretting that it would get crushed in transit and bringing it out for frequent airings. By the time they reached Toronto, Betty Somervell was exhausted.

It was typical of Grey Owl that he gave little thought to the demands he made on those around him. It may partly have been that the demands that he placed upon himself were enormous and so he thought nothing of imposing similar standards on others. It may also have been that he was just never very good at looking after the people close to him. He had abandoned Angele, Marie, and Ivy; Agnes, Johnny, and Flora. He had shared much with Anahareo but eventually withdrew even from her. His caring and empathy he devoted to causes beyond the personal, where the risk of immediate rejection was less and the rewards, in the form of attention, were greater. And because the character paraded on the public stage was not who he really was, even if he were to be rejected here, the rejection would be of the persona and not of the man beneath.

Grey Owl spent some time in Toronto in spring of 1936 on his return from Great Britain. He was interviewed by the media and caused a stir with his remarks on religion. He believed that Christianity—unlike Buddhism, for example—failed to emphasize tolerance for so-called lower forms of life. He also believed that the religions of North American Indians were more suited to their way of life and that it was arrogant to impose Christianity upon them.

In Toronto, he met up with two people who had known him before he became a celebrity: Arthur Stevens, the justice of the peace to whom he had applied for a license to marry Angele and to whom Ivy Holmes had sent her divorce papers, and Donalda Legace, daughter of the woman who had run the boardinghouse in Biscotasing. Although both knew many details of Grey Owl's past, neither wished to say anything that might interfere with the work he was doing. It must have been clear to Grey Owl, however, how easy it would be for his cover to be blown. This knowledge could not have done much for his state of mind. As his Canadian publisher, Hugh Eayrs, wrote to Lovat Dickson: "He is, not to put too fine a point on it, quite scared of meeting people here in Toronto."

Grey Owl did make one chance encounter that he welcomed. He had left Toronto for Ottawa to meet with the governor-general and the prime minister. One morning, in a restaurant near his hotel, he ran into John Tootoosis, a young Plains Cree from Saskatchewan who was a great-nephew of Chief Poundmaker. Tootoosis was in Ottawa to plead with the federal government for a more humane Indian policy. Grey Owl immediately invited him to use his room at the Plaza Hotel if he needed somewhere to rest for the day and made introductions for him at the Department of Indian Affairs. Tootoosis was not taken in by Grey Owl's Indian persona, but he recognized in him someone who had a genuine sympathy for Indians in Canada and who was willing to do what he could to help ameliorate their situation.

Grey Owl lingered in Toronto on the way home rather than rushing back to be with Anahareo and Dawn. When he did eventually return, it was to see his daughter, who was in hospital in

Prince Albert with pneumonia. Perhaps one reason for his reluctance to return was Alexandra Dick, an attractive young woman who had trailed after him during his lecture tour of England.

When Grey Owl returned to Saskatchewan from Toronto in late March, he went on a drinking spree in Prince Albert and had a huge row with Anahareo, who, it seemed, then made a final decision to leave him. After the row, Anahareo decided to spend the summer at Waskesiu with Dawn. She returned to Beaver Lodge just once more, in September to seek comfort from Grey Owl after she had witnessed the drowning of one of the park wardens.

Before Grey Owl had left Ottawa he had met with the governor-general, Lord Tweedsmuir, to try to secure funding for a film he wished to make of the Mississagi River country where he had worked as a fire ranger in the early 1920s. He worried about the effect of logging on the vast pine forests of northern Ontario, and he wanted the area to be declared a park before it was too late.

*Facing page:* Grey Owl was greeted on his return from his first British tour in 1936 as an international celebrity. He sat for a portrait with the renowned photographer Yousuf Karsh and lobbied Canadian government officials in support of his conservationist cause.

For Grey Owl, the Mississagi River country was a symbol of the Canadian wilderness, and he worked hard to broadcast its importance to the world. Lord Tweedsmuir, the former John Buchan, was a highly successful author himself and a great admirer of Grey Owl's writing. Grey Owl also lobbied Prime Minister Mackenzie King, who had been instrumental in the establishment of Prince Albert National Park; and the minister of the interior, Tom Crerar, whose department

would have some say in the matter. While Grey Owl was in Ottawa lobbying for his cause, he took time off to visit his old friend Lloyd Roberts, son of the famous man of letters Sir Charles G. D. Roberts. Lloyd had first met Grey Owl in Cabano and had then visited with him in Riding Mountain National Park. In Ottawa, Roberts introduced Grey Owl to an attractive French-Canadian woman named Yvonne Perrier.

*Facing page:* Anahareo had become frustrated with Grey Owl's devoted attention to his books. At first she had escaped by going prospecting in the North. Then, in 1936, when it seemed clear he would never change, she left him for good.

During Grey Owl's visit, the Ottawa photographer Yousuf Karsh arranged a party for Grey Owl to meet several influential people. Unfortunately, that night Grey Owl was to be found in an inebriated state in the bar of the Plaza Hotel. Karsh, who had gone out in search of his guest of honor, decided it was best to leave him there.

Grey Owl's refuge in alcohol as he recovered from his strenuous British tour and plucked up the courage to return to Anahareo and Dawn did not help his effort to raise money for his film. News of his drinking traveled back to government circles; he retained his position with the Parks Branch but lost hope of government backing for his film.

After the break with Anahareo, Grey Owl found himself increasingly frustrated with life at Beaver Lodge. He crammed his days with writing, perhaps to replace the vigorous outdoor activities that once had been part of his daily life and from which he had drawn so much satisfaction. He seemed to think that if

# The Mississagi River

*Grey Owl lobbied to preserve the pine forests of northern Ontario,
and his film of the Mississagi River was just one of the ways in which
he brought this area to the attention of the world.*

WE PASS SEVERAL small lake expansions, and that night we camp beside swiftly running water, on the banks of the River proper. And all night, whenever we awaken, we can hear, in the distance, a dull, steady, ceaseless roar. Our first real white water, with all its unknown possibilities, lies just ahead of us. The next morning we arrive at the head of this. Part of the load is disembarked at the portage, as we will run with half loads, taking only stuff that can stand a wetting. For this is a tough spot, and we will ship water, inevitably. We go to [the] centre of the stream again, set the canoes at the proper angle for the take-off. The canoes seem to leap suddenly ahead, and one after another, with a wild, howling hurrah, we are into the thick of it. Huge combers, any one of which would swamp a canoe, stand reared and birling terrifically beside us, close enough to touch. The backlash from one of these smashes against the bows and we are slashed in the face by what seems to be a ton of water; we are soaked to the skin, blinded by spray—on one side is a solid wall of water, there is a thunderous roar which envelopes us like it was a tunnel, a last

*Facing page:* Grey Owl's fourth wife, Yvonne Perrier, was with him when he made a film to publicize the Mississagi River, on which he had spent so many happy days fire-ranging in his youth.

flying leap and we are in the still pool below, safe, set, and thrilled to the bone.... We go ashore, unload and empty out, carry the remaining stuff over the portage, load up and are away again....

And as we penetrate deeper and ever deeper into this enchanted land, the River marches with us. More and more to us a living thing, it sometimes seems as if it were watching us, like some huge half-sleeping serpent that observes us dreamily, lying there secure in his consciousness of power while we, like Lilliputians, play perilously upon his back.

Facing page: Unable to get government backing for the Mississagi River film, Grey Owl hired independent Ontario filmmaker Bert Bach.

Here and there along its course are mighty waterfalls, some with rainbows at the foot of them; and one of these thunders down a deep chasm, down two hundred feet into a dark swirling eddy, seemingly bottomless, that heaves and boils below the beetling overhang as though some unimaginably monstrous creature moved beneath its surface. And in the vortex of this boiling cauldron there stands a pinnacle of rock on which no creature ever stood, crowned with a single tree, forever wet with the rainbow-tinted spray that in a mist hangs over it, while the echoing, red walls of the gorge and the crest of the looming pines that overtop them, and the all-surrounding amphitheatre of the hills, throw back and forth in thunderous repetition the awe-inspiring reverberations of the mighty cataract. And as we stand and watch it, it is borne home to us what a really little figure a man cuts in this great Wilderness.

he made the film he would get the opportunity to test himself against nature and see if he still measured up. The wilderness was a place where he had proved his worth as a young man. Was he worth as much now as he had been before he met Anahareo, or were those days lost to him forever? In mid-May he learned that his request for government funding towards his film project had been turned down.

With the film project temporarily on hold, Grey Owl immersed himself in the manuscript for *Tales of an Empty Cabin*. Mrs. Winters's teenaged children, Stan and Margaret, came up to the lodge to lend a hand. Margaret typed the manuscript and Stan looked after the beavers. Over seven hundred visitors also came to be shown around. The first draft of the manuscript was completed by mid-August. The tone of the book is nostalgic, and Grey Owl seems to be reminiscing about good times lost rather than building for the future.

His writing commitments completed, Grey Owl traveled with his daughter Dawn to Fort Carlton to join the various Indian groups celebrating the sixtieth anniversary of the signing of Treaty 6. Lord Tweedsmuir was also in attendance. Grey Owl contributed to the dancing in his imitation of Indian style, and after Lord Tweedsmuir had left he pledged to the Indians assembled that he would do whatever he could to further their cause. The Indians knew he wasn't really one of them but did not expose him because they appreciated his efforts on their behalf. As for Grey Owl, he seemed to believe that they were convinced of his authenticity. The trip revitalized him, and he expressed to Superintendent of Parks Jim Wood his intention to carry out more public work if permitted.

In late September 1936, Betty Somervell visited Grey Owl at Beaver Lodge. Anahareo was also there. Lord Tweedsmuir dropped by for an afternoon, and Grey Owl told him of his view that Indians could play an important role in the economic future of Canada as stewards of the wilderness. Anahareo stayed for a while, perhaps trying to recapture something of the relationship she and Grey Owl had once shared. Resigning herself to the fact that he was not going to change, she left him for the last time that fall and never saw him again.

When it was clear that the rift with Anahareo was irrevocable, Grey Owl seemed bound and determined to find another woman with whom to share his life. In mid-September Alexandra Dick informed him that she had decided against coming out to Saskatchewan. He turned his attentions to Olga Pavlova in Regina. Olga was in her mid-twenties, a professional singer by night and a clerk at Simpson's by day. By early November he was set on marrying her. She must have turned him down, but he did have dinner with her the next year when he lectured in Regina shortly before his death. Single-minded as ever, he wrote to Yvonne Perrier to let her know he would like to see her when he came to Ottawa after attending the Toronto Book Fair in early November.

No other author equaled Grey Owl for crowd appeal at Canada's first book fair. Seventeen hundred people crowded the

King Edward Hotel's Crystal Ballroom to hear him speak on November 9; five hundred would-be spectators were turned away. On November 10 he addressed a lunch at the Women's Press Club in Eaton's, the site of his first job in Canada, an irony that was probably not lost on him. On November 11 he was back at the book fair. On November 12 he addressed Toronto's Empire Club. Then it was off to Ottawa to visit Yvonne.

Grey Owl proposed to Yvonne in late November. Perhaps he knew that in his precarious mental state he needed a steadying influence, someone to look after him when the stress of acting out his role and presenting his message to the world overcame him. Little knowing what she was letting herself in for as the wife of this tireless and demanding man, Yvonne accepted his proposal and resigned her position as a lady's companion on November 30.

*Facing page:* French-Canadian Yvonne Perrier resigned her position as a lady's companion in 1936 to marry Grey Owl. She had no idea of his true identity and no idea of the breakneck pace at which she was to live for the next eighteen months of her life.

To avoid complications because of his marriage to Angele, Grey Owl married Yvonne under the name of McNeil rather than Belaney, even though he was known to the Parks Branch as Archie Belaney. How he thought this new strand in his life story would simplify matters is not clear. He shared little of his past with Yvonne, and she believed his stories of an Apache mother and a Scottish father, with some details added to explain his new last name. After they were married, Grey Owl and Yvonne traveled to Montreal and Toronto, arriving at Beaver Lodge on New Year's Day 1937.

In 1937, Grey Owl desperately wanted to make two films: one of the Abitibi region in winter and one of the Mississagi River in summer. Both were to immortalize "the wilderness," to present its soul before it vanished before the onslaught of development. After the setback with the Mississagi film, Grey Owl reached an agreement with his Canadian and British publishers that they would pay for the winter film in Abitibi, since he was to use it in lecture tours to promote his books. Grey Owl hired cameraman Bert Bach to shoot the picture.

*Facing page:* The film of winter in Abitibi brought Grey Owl back to his days on the trap line when he would snowshoe for miles, eschewing the use of dogs and pulling his sleds himself. It was clear from the film, however, that by 1937 his physical strength was fast waning.

In March 1937, in an interview with the North Bay *Nugget* before shooting the Abitibi film, Grey Owl learned, to his great consternation, that the newspaper knew who he was. In 1935 the newspaper had followed a tip to Angele in Temagami, who had told them that Grey Owl was her husband, Archie Belaney. Grey Owl's reaction to this news during the interview seemed to confirm the story. The paper, however, did not publish the findings, which would have been sure to derail the work that Grey Owl was undertaking to preserve the Canadian wilderness. Instead, the *Nugget's* editor and his reporter held on to their story and did not publish it until the day after Grey Owl's death the following year.

The Abitibi film was completed in March, and Grey Owl went on a drinking binge in Toronto when it was over. He was drunk through most of the two-week editing process and Yvonne had her hands full looking after him. Although the film contained impressive scenes of Grey Owl traveling on snowshoes, camping out in winter, and driving a dog team, it was obvious from the completed footage that he was in poor health and his physical strength was on the wane. He may also have felt that it was now only a matter of time before his true identity would be revealed.

In April, Grey Owl and Yvonne were back in Beaver Lodge. Despite his failing strength, he was working at a breakneck pace. Perhaps he sensed that time was running out, and now that he had the attention of the world, there was so much that he wanted to achieve. That spring he wrote captions for the Abitibi film and drew sketches for a reprint of one of his stories, *The Tree*, which Lovat Dickson wanted to bring out in book form. Grey Owl had no financial help from his publishers for the summer film. He decided to press ahead anyway and foot the bill himself. Once again, he hired Bert Bach.

*Facing page:* Grey Owl particularly enjoyed being recognized by the North American Indian community. In 1937 he joined other Indians at Niagara Falls to celebrate their right to cross the border between Canada and the United States without restriction.

Grey Owl and Yvonne arrived in Biscotasing, the jumping-off point for the summer film, in early June. Grey Owl took the opportunity to look up old friends, among them Jimmy and Jane Espaniel and the retired manager of the Hudson's Bay Company post, Harry Woodworth. Jimmy and Jane broke the news to Grey Owl that their father, Alex Espaniel, had died the previous year. Grey Owl was devastated that he had been denied a chance to say goodbye to the man who had been like a father to him.

# A MESSAGE OF CONSERVATION

*Grey Owl devoted his lectures to raising people's awareness that if they did not act, the wilderness would disappear. Nature was not something that could be taken for granted.*

TOO MANY REGARD the wilderness as only a place of wild animals and wilder men, and cluttered with a growth that must somehow be got rid of. Yet it is, to those who know its ways, a living, breathing reality, and has a soul that may be understood, and it may yet occur to some, that part of the duty of those who destroy it for the general good is to preserve at least a memory of it and its inhabitants, and what they stood for.

*Facing page: "Far enough away to gain seclusion, yet within reach of those whose genuine interest prompts them to make the trip, Beaver Lodge extends a welcome to you if your heart is right."*

The Wilderness should now no longer be considered as a playground for vandals, or a rich treasure trove to be ruthlessly exploited for the personal gains of the few—to be grabbed off by whoever happens to get there first.

If you had seen, as I have, noble forests reduced in a few hours to arid deserts sparsely dotted with the twisted, tortured skeletons of what once were trees, things of living beauty, (or if you are very practically minded, things of high value), excuse could no doubt be found for my zeal.

The Provinces of Canada have at last decided, now that some varieties of animals and timber are on the point of disappearance, to get together and try to evolve some means of preserving Canada's rapidly dwindling natural forest resources. The stable door is about to be closed, the horse having long gone. How slowly we move!

I make no false claims that I am out especially to try and do the public good, or that I have some "message" for the world. I am only trying to do what little is within my power for those

creatures amongst whom my life has been passed. And if by
so doing I can also be of some little service to my fellow-man,
the opportunity becomes a two-fold privilege. I do not
expect to accomplish much in the short span
that is left to me, but hope to assist, even if only
in a minor role, in laying a foundation on which
abler hands and better heads may later build.
In this way I may perhaps be instrumental, at
least to some extent, in the work of saving from
entire destruction some of those interesting
and useful dwellers in our waste places, in
whom lie unexpected possibilities that await
but a little kindness and understanding to develop the rank
and file of that vast, inarticulate army of living creatures from
whom we can never hear.

*Facing page:* From the tranquillity of Ajawaan, Grey Owl wrote: "Remember you belong to Nature, not it to you." When he toured, people always asked about Anahareo, his first audience and the woman who had set him on his conservationist path.

So let not those who are benefiting by the prosperity of the
present day forget the debt they owe to the Life of the Wild; the
part it has played in the progress of the country in the past and its
immense (potential) value in the industries and recreation of the
present and, let us hope, the future. It is no longer a matter, as it
was twenty years ago, of slaughtering off as large a quantity of
game as possible just to see in how many different ways a stricken
animal may hit the ground. Things are different now, and the
time will come when a well-taken photograph will be a greater
test of a good hunter than the possession of the head or hide.

Grey Owl was fond of Jane and asked her what she thought of his books. She knew that Grey Owl was really Archie Belaney, but she did not begrudge him his fame and success. When she was a child, he had always been good to her, so she just told him: "I can't spin long tales like you do. To me it's just a lot of north wind blowing." She helped him with the ritual of dyeing his hair black and reminisced with him about old times. No one said anything about his reworked identity as Grey Owl; no one wanted to take away from all that he had achieved in his assumed role.

After the Mississagi River film was completed, Grey Owl put on one of his trademark war dances in Bisco before returning to Toronto to edit the footage. While he was in Toronto the Indian Defense League of America invited him to the border crossing at Niagara to celebrate the right of North American Indians to cross the international border unrestricted. It was the first time the man who claimed to have grown up in the American Southwest had ever set foot on American soil, and it was at this event that Yvonne was given the name Silver Moon by an Iroquois.

From Niagara, Grey Owl and Yvonne traveled to a meeting of the Brampton council of the Indian Association of America to celebrate the induction of four new members. Grey Owl and Yvonne then went back to Beaver Lodge before traveling to North Battleford in early August to open the town's annual fair. Then they returned to Beaver Lodge to work on Grey Owl's costume for his second British tour. It was to be even more elaborate and heavily beaded than the outfit he had worn on his previous visit across the Atlantic. Meanwhile, Grey Owl's Canadian publisher, Macmillan, prepared an anthology of his writings, to be called *A Book of Grey Owl*, and over one thousand visitors came to Beaver Lodge.

In September of 1937, Grey Owl and Yvonne left for England on the ss *Montrose*. The manager of this tour was Ken Conibear, a young Canadian who had grown up in the North and who had studied at Oxford University as a Rhodes Scholar. To avoid disappointing audiences who still thought of Anahareo as Grey Owl's partner, Grey Owl presented Yvonne as his secretary. It was Ken and Yvonne's job to ensure that Grey Owl got to his lectures on time and to keep him as sober as possible. From September 27 to October 23, Grey Owl gave fifty performances at the Polytechnic Theatre in London before traveling through the rest of the country. Despite his precarious mental and physical states, Grey Owl performed superbly. Each presentation was unique; each was spellbinding.

Grey Owl had seen his aunts on his first tour of Great Britain, and on this tour he met with them again. He also saw his mother, who came to visit him on November 30, 1937, in the Mitre Hotel in Oxford. Yvonne was unaware of the relationship between the two, and she left the room soon after Kittie arrived. That night Kittie came to hear her son lecture, and he gave an unusually lackluster performance, probably thrown off kilter by his mother's presence.

On December 10, 1937, Grey Owl gave a command performance at Buckingham Palace to King George vi, Queen Elizabeth, and Princesses Elizabeth and Margaret. Grey Owl, true to form, did things his way. He refused to observe royal protocol and insisted that the audience be seated before he entered the

room. After the lecture he spoke informally with the king about the need for conservation. When he left, he reached out to the king, touched him on the shoulder, and called him brother.

Five days later, Grey Owl was in the sitting room of Aunts Carrie and Ada in Hastings. The night before he had lectured at the White Rock Pavilion. In the audience was Mary McCormick, the sister of his childhood friend George McCormick. Mary was sure she recognized Archie, but she went no further than confiding her suspicions to another boyhood friend of Archie's. She told him: "That's Archie Belaney or I'll eat my hat." Once again Yvonne had no idea of the connection between Grey Owl and the two old ladies he visited. Once again Grey Owl had narrowly escaped being unmasked by someone familiar with his past.

*Facing page:* Grey Owl returned to Britain one last time in 1937. The crowning glory of the tour was an audience with King George VI and his family. Grey Owl traveled with a sun lamp to keep his skin tanned, and Yvonne dyed his hair black every two weeks.

The tour ended with a lecture in London on December 18 and what was to be a farewell broadcast on *Children's Hour* on the British Broadcasting Corporation on December 20. The broadcast was never made, because Grey Owl had spoken out against fox hunting in the script he had sent to the broadcaster for approval. The BBC would not allow criticism of the sport unless both sides of the issue could be aired, and Grey Owl, with characteristic stubbornness, would not change his text. Lovat Dickson published the text in pamphlet form instead and also included it in a tribute to Grey Owl published just after his death entitled *The Green Leaf.*

Grey Owl and Yvonne sailed back to North America on December 21 on the ss *Berengaria*. When they arrived in New York, Grey Owl embarked on yet another lecture tour, making numerous crossings of the border from the United States to Canada over the next three months. Grey Owl was less successful in the United States than he had been in Great Britain. Perhaps elaborately outfitted Indians were less of a novelty in America than they were in Britain, or maybe Grey Owl understood less about the expectations of the American public. Whatever the reason, his performance was disappointing. The circumstances surrounding his tour were discouraging also. At the outset he had trouble getting U.S. customs officials to believe that he had been born in Mexico and raised in Arizona. Then *Time* magazine seemed as interested in juicy details about his personal life as it was in his conservationist message, reporting that he had been married twice legally and five times according to Indian lore. To top it all off, his editor at Scribner's, Maxwell Perkins, did not meet with him when he visited the publishing house and did not attend Grey Owl's first lecture in New York.

Grey Owl received a warmer welcome in Canada. Canadians seemed to feel now that he had proven himself elsewhere, he could be hailed as a celebrity in his adopted country. He traveled extensively in Ontario and Quebec. On this, his last tour, he concentrated especially on the children. In Peterborough

*Facing page:* Especially in his later years, Grey Owl delighted in speaking to children. Here he is towards the end of his final tour talking to a group of schoolchildren in Windsor, Ontario. He always hoped that others would continue with his message after he was gone.

he was photographed visiting a young amputee in hospital; in Windsor he spoke to several thousand children in over twenty schools. Grey Owl once again met with Tom Crerar, now minister of mines and natural resources, in Ottawa. He spoke to him about the need to provide Canadian Indians with better health services and opportunities to continue their traditional way of life.

On his tour, he met up again with Jean-Charles Harvey, the journalist who had given him his first break in the media; with Haddow Keith, who had been a fire ranger with him on the Mississagi after the war; and with Mrs. Madeline Peck, who had arranged that first lecture in Métis in 1929. Grey Owl continued to deliver his conservationist message, urging Canadians not to squander their natural resources and to show respect for the animals and the people with whom they shared their country.

Grey Owl's final appearance in eastern Canada was in Massey Hall, Toronto, on March 26, 1938. After traveling seventeen hours, he had just two hours to prepare for a lecture to a crowd of nearly three thousand. Once again, he rose to the occasion, enchanting everyone for two hours. He was then rushed onto another train for his final lecture, in Regina, on March 29.

By the time Grey Owl and Yvonne reached Prince Albert in early April, Yvonne was so exhausted that she was sent to a hospital in Regina. Grey Owl continued on to Beaver Lodge. He reached the cabin on April 7. Three days later, he contacted the Parks Branch in Waskesiu by radio telephone to let them know that he was not feeling well. A park warden brought him by dog sled from Ajawaan to Kingsmere Lake, where a truck was waiting to take him to Waskesiu. From there he was driven to the hospital in Prince Albert. He seemed to do well for a couple of days, and then suddenly he got a fever. Within twelve hours, he was dead. He had a slight touch of pneumonia, but in his worn-out state, that was enough to kill him. Anahareo was in Prince Albert the day he died, but she had not visited him because she had not realized the seriousness of his condition.

On hearing of Grey Owl's death, the editor of the North Bay *Nugget* immediately ran his story. A media uproar ensued in which the merits of the man and his message were hotly debated. Was his crusade to save the wilderness he loved any less sincere because he was not the man he claimed to be? If he were an impostor, could his words be sincere? After the initial furor had died down, it was up to posterity to decide on the merits of his case.

It is the mix of sincerity and intrigue that has kept Grey Owl's legacy alive. He was ahead of his time, speaking out on issues of conservation that would not enter the popular consciousness until the 1970s and on Native rights that only today are being given widespread attention. We remember him in part because his message is still relevant today and in part because of his marvelous sleight of hand, leading to the detective work required to reconcile his public and private personas. Perhaps there is an element of awe as well. In the last decade of his life, the lonely English schoolboy did what many of us can only yearn to do: he lived his dream and the world took note.

# PRESS COMMENTARY

*After Grey Owl's death, the media were divided as to whether it mattered that he had delivered his conservationist message under an assumed identity. The consensus was that the importance of his message transcended his deception and his choice of persona ensured that his words were heard by the widest audience possible.*

WHO GREY OWL was at his birth seems to be the great question; whether he was a clever schoolboy at Hastings with a passion for animals and Red Indian life, or the son of a Scotsman who had been an Indian Scout with an Apache mother. There is romance in either case for people with sympathy and imagination, for the thing that really matters about a man is where he is going to, and not so much where he came from.

*Facing page: Grey Owl always believed that people could achieve anything they set out to do provided that they tried hard and were sincere. He certainly persevered in times of adversity, and the sincerity of his message assured him of a wide and loyal following.*

The chances are that Archie Belaney could not have done nearly such effective work for conservation of wild life under his own name. It is an odd commentary, but true enough, that many people will not listen to simple truths except when buffered by exotic personalities.

What, after all, does his ancestry matter? The essential facts about his life are not in dispute, for as conservation officer under the Canadian Government, and as lecturer and Broadcaster in

Great Britain, he worked unceasingly for the protection of wild life. This work, and, in particular, his efforts on behalf of the beaver colonies in Canada, gained him the popular title of 'ambassador from the wild'. When a man has devoted his best years to such a cause it is surely unfair that he should be dubbed an 'impostor' because he may, if certain evidence is correct, have been an Englishman and not a Red Indian. Those who have read Grey Owl's books or heard his broadcasts cannot doubt his sincerity, and the record of his work speaks for itself. In these circumstances it would seem that Grey Owl should be accepted for the nature-lover which he undoubtedly was, and that controversy over his ancestry may be dismissed as unnecessary gossip.

*Facing page:* Grey Owl was a storyteller with a flair for the dramatic who believed that he could make a difference to the way that people viewed nature. His views are as relevant today as they were when he promoted them in the 1930s.

The world is ready to forget the private lives of Burns, Shelley, Byron, Marlowe, Verlaine, Swinburn, Rossetti. The beauty of their work lives on.

So it should be with Grey Owl. He preached a gospel of tolerance towards the animal world, not for sentimental reasons, but because, as he said, 'It is just sense.'

He will be freely extended the tolerance he preached by all who remember with gratitude that he was a man who had the courage to tell the civilized world that it still had much to learn.

# $\mathcal{A}$CKNOWLEDGMENTS

MY THANKS TO Rob Sanders at Greystone Books for suggesting this book, and to Nancy Flight for her perceptive editorial comments. Thanks to Christine Bourolias at the Archives of Ontario and Judith Graham at Prince Albert National Park for their help with photo research. Most especially I thank Don Smith, whose book, *From the Land of Shadows*, provided much of the information in this book. Don was also kind enough to read a draft of this manuscript and to give me encouragement throughout the project. Any errors of fact or interpretation that remain are mine.

# References

BOOKS BY GREY OWL

*The Men of the Last Frontier.* London: Country Life, 1931.

*Pilgrims of the Wild.* Toronto: Macmillan, 1934.

*The Adventures of Sajo and Her Beaver People.* London: Lovat Dickson & Thompson Limited, 1935. (Published by Macmillan Canada and Scribner's in the United States as *Sajo and the Beaver People.*)

*Tales of an Empty Cabin.* London: Lovat Dickson Limited, 1936.

*The Tree.* London: Lovat Dickson Limited, 1937. (Previously published as a chapter in *Tales of an Empty Cabin.*)

*A Book of Grey Owl: Pages from the Writings of Wa-Sha-Quon-Asin.* E. E. Reynolds, ed. London: Peter Davies, 1938.

BOOKS ABOUT GREY OWL

Anahareo. *My Life with Grey Owl.* London: Peter Davies, 1940.

Anahareo. *Devil in Deerskins. My Life with Grey Owl.* Toronto: New Press, 1972.

Dickson, Lovat. *Half-Breed: The Story of Grey Owl.* London: Peter Davies, 1939.

Dickson, Lovat. *Wilderness Man: The Strange Story of Grey Owl.* Toronto: Macmillan, 1973.

Dickson, Lovat, ed. *The Green Leaf. A Tribute to Grey Owl.* London: Lovat Dickson Limited, 1938.

Ruffo, Armand Garnet. *Grey Owl: The Mystery of Archie Belaney.* Regina, Saskatchewan: Coteau Books, 1996.

Smith, Donald B. *From the Land of Shadows: The Making of Grey Owl.* Saskatoon, Saskatchewan: Western Producer Prairie Books, 1990. Reprint, Vancouver, B.C.: Greystone Books, 1999.

# Notes

*The numbers on the left refer to page numbers.*

1  "How did the soul . . . ?" Mary McCormick, *West Australia*,
   April 20, 1938.

9  "Indians of the type . . ." *Hastings & St. Leonards Observer*,
   August 22, 1903.

10  "Neganikabo, my mentor . . ." *Men of the Last Frontier*, pp. 227–28.

13  "I buried him the next day. . . ." *Men of the Last Frontier*, p. 247.

16  "Oh no, Archie . . ." Quoted in Eva-Lis Wuorio, "Grey Owl's
    Widow Gives Happy Hilarity to Camp," Toronto *Globe and Mail*,
    July 24, 1947.

20  "And as I sit . . ." *Tales of an Empty Cabin*, p. 162.

20  "So, speed, speed, speed . . ." *Tales of an Empty Cabin*, p. 182.

23  "The spruce trees look like . . ." *Tales of an Empty Cabin*, p. 217.

23  "And down its mad course . . ." *Tales of an Empty Cabin*, p. 221.

24  ". . . murder the beautiful . . ." "An Old Hastonian amongst the
    Indians," *The Hastonian*, number 10 ( July 1914), pp. 5–7.

26  ". . . considered a white man . . ." J. W. Cowper, "Grey Owl in Ontario,"
    Letter to the Editor, Toronto *Globe and Mail*, April 28, 1938.

30  "Beautiful as this Arctic forest appears . . ." *Men of the Last Frontier*,
    pp. 43–44.

38  "He who leads . . ." *Men of the Last Frontier*, pp. 6–7.

38  "In tune with . . ." *Men of the Last Frontier*, p. 8.

41  "He scans the face of . . ." *Men of the Last Frontier*, p. 20.

41  "An anachronism . . ." *Men of the Last Frontier*, p. 25.

43  ". . . the one I am proud to call 'Dad.'" Inscription in the copy of
    *Pilgrims of the Wild* Archie sent to Alex Espaniel.

47    "... *son inspiratrice*..." Jean-Charles Harvey, "Grey Owl est Mort,"
       *Le Jour* (Montreal), April 23, 1938.

48    "Say, do you happen ..." Anahareo, *Devil in Deerskins*, p. 2.

49    "After five hours of snowshoeing..." Anahareo, *Devil in
       Deerskins*, p. 15.

54    "The canoe became quickly coated ..." *Pilgrims of the Wild*, pp. 85–88.

54    "their rollicking good fellowship," "child-like intimacies." *Pilgrims of
       the Wild*, p. 53.

58    "Good old Anahareo ..." *Pilgrims of the Wild*, p. 55.

59    "I am now..." *Pilgrims of the Wild*, p. 54.

62    "On Christmas Eve all was ready..." *Pilgrims of the Wild*, pp. 144–46.

69    "... felt a good deal like ..." *Pilgrims of the Wild*, p. 175.

70    "When she was on the bunk ..." *Pilgrims of the Wild*, p. 208.

71    "... a living argument ..." G. M. Dallyn to Donald B. Smith, cited in
       *From the Land of Shadows*, p. 89.

72    "In this creature there was life ..." *Pilgrims of the Wild*, pp. 197–98.

72    "Any branches brought in for feed ..." *Pilgrims of the Wild*, p. 194.

75    "Her attempts at communication ..." *Pilgrims of the Wild*, pp. 197–98.

75    "... the same air..." *Tales of an Empty Cabin*, p. 313.

79    "Far below..." *Pilgrims of the Wild*, p. 99.

81    "Ajawaan; a small, deep lake ..." *Tales of an Empty Cabin*, p. 281.

85    "We are lucky..." W. G. N. van der Sleen. *Canada*. Tilburg:
       Nederland's Boekhuis, 1947, pp. 162–63, passage translated by
       Laurie Meijer-Dreis.

86    "This whiskey-jack ..." *Men of the Last Frontier.* pp. 14–15.

86    "The most resplendent ..." *Tales of an Empty Cabin*, p. 285.

89    "It is no uncommon thing ..." *Tales of an Empty Cabin*, p. 275.

89    "After a while ..." *Tales of an Empty Cabin*, p. 73.

90    "Pride forbids ..." *Tales of an Empty Cabin*, p. 77.

90    "As I was making my preparations..." *Tales of an Empty Cabin*, p. 293.

90 "She lies there . . ." *Tales of an Empty Cabin*, p. 311.

94 ". . . assumed the Red Brother . . ." W. A. Deacon to Grey Owl, April 24, 1935. William Arthur Deacon Papers, Thomas Fisher Rare Book Library, University of Toronto.

98 "Gray Owl steps right out of . . ." M. H. Halton, "Grey Owl Seeing London Has Trapped Animal Feeling," *Toronto Star*, February 13, 1936.

98 "My heart sank . . ." Geoffrey Turner, diary entry, January 24, 1936. Cited in *From the Land of Shadows*, p. 125.

101 "[Grey Owl] made pure Canada . . ." Lovat Dickson, *Wilderness Man*, pp. 239–40.

102 "Indians are in tune with . . ." *Men of the Last Frontier*, p. 219.

103 "We must not fail to remember . . ." *Men of the Last Frontier*, p. 151.

103 "The Indian is not to be . . ." Grey Owl to John Tootoosis, reporting a conversation with the governor-general of Canada, Lord Tweedsmuir, at Lake Ajawaan in the fall of 1936. H. J. Fraser Papers, Saskatchewan Archives Board, Saskatoon, Saskatchewan.

105 "I have a very deep affection for him . . ." Lovat Dickson to Hugh Eayrs, London, January 19, 1936. Macmillan Archive, The William Ready Division of Archives and Research Collections, McMaster University Library, Hamilton, Ontario.

105 "In G.O.'s room . . ." Betty Somervell, diary entry for February 25, 1936. Copy in Donald B. Smith, Grey Owl Collection, Glenbow Archives, Calgary, Canada.

107 "He is, not to put too fine a point on it . . ." Hugh Eayrs to Lovat Dickson, Toronto, March 9, 1936. Macmillan Archive, The William Ready Division of Archives and Research Collections, McMaster University Library, Hamilton, Ontario.

112 "We pass several small lake expansions . . ." *Tales of an Empty Cabin*, pp. 206–7.

115   "And as we penetrate deeper..." *Tales of an Empty Cabin*, p. 213.

115   "Here and there along its course..." *Tales of an Empty Cabin*, p. 214.

122   "I can't spin long tales..." Interview with Jane Espaniel McKee with Donald B. Smith, Toronto, September 29, 1987. Cited in *From the Land of Shadows*, p. 177.

124   "Too many regard the wilderness..." *Men of the Last Frontier*, p. 171.

124   "The Wilderness should now no longer be..." *Tales of an Empty Cabin*, p. vii.

124   "If you had seen..." *Men of the Last Frontier*, p. 174.

124   "Far enough away..." *Tales of an Empty Cabin*, p. 274.

126   "The Provinces of Canada have at last decided..." *Men of the Last Frontier*, p. 218.

126   "I make no false claims..." *Pilgrims of the Wild*, p. 332.

127   "So let not those..." *The Illustrated Canadian Forest and Outdoors*, March 1931, p. 121.

127   "Remember..." Grey Owl, Notebook 'A' 1936, Grey Owl Collection, MG30, D 237, National Archives of Canada.

131   "That's Archie..." *Evening Argus*, 1937

136   "Who Grey Owl was..." *The Star*, April 20, 1938.

136   "The chances are..." *Winnipeg Tribune*, April 10, 1938.

136   "What, after all..." *Liverpool Daily Post*, April 21, 1938.

139   "The world is ready to forget..." *Daily Herald*, April 21, 1938.

# $\mathcal{P}$HOTO CREDITS